First published 2021

(c) 2021 Dominic Salles

All rights reserved. The right of Dominic Salles to be identified as th
asserted by them in accordance with the Copyright, Designs and Pat
work may be reproduced, stored in a retrieval system, transmitted in any form or by any means, electronical, mechanical, photocopying, recording, or otherwise, without the prior permission of the Author.

Dominic Salles still lives in Swindon, with his workaholic wife Deirdre, his jiu-jitsu-loving engineer son, Harry, and Bob, the 16.5-year-old rescue dog who refuses to die. Both of them are leaving soon – one way or another.

His daughter is educating students in Wales because, now Brexit is done, Brussels isn't stepping in to help the Welsh any more. Cardiff is awesome.

His sister Jacey is famous for her Spanish accent, on your TV screens. She would be hilarious in her own YouTube channel. He still drives a 2006 Prius.

His YouTube channel, Mr Salles Teaches English, will one day earn him a living. Even if it doesn't, he is still going snowboarding for three months in January 2021 because it is the cheapest and healthiest midlife crisis he can imagine.

Contents

Copyright	Page 1
Author Biography	Page 1
Contents	Page 2
Introduction	Page 4
The Structure	Page 5
Ebenezer Scrooge	Page 8
Bob Cratchit	Page 24
Fred	Page 31
Jacob Marley	Page 35
Ghost of Christmas Past	Page 40
Ghost of Christmas Present	Page 44
Ghost of Christmas Yet to Come	Page 50
Tiny Tim	Page 54
The Narrator	Page 58
Belle	Page 63
Context	Page 66
Themes: Social Dissatisfaction and the Poor Laws	Page 75
Theme and Context of Poverty	Page 78
Theme of Generosity	Page 79
Theme of Greed	Page 84
Theme of Regret	Page 88
Theme of Moral Responsibility	Page 91
Theme of the Christmas Spirit	Page 95

Theme of Winter and the Mythology of Christmas	Page 97
Theme of Family	Page 99
Theme of Redemption	Page 102
Theme of Time	Page 105
Grade 9 Essays	Page 108
How is A Christmas Carol a Criticism of Social Policy in Victorian England?	Page 108
How Does Dickens Use the Ghosts in A Christmas Carol?	Page 110
What is the importance of family in A Christmas Carol?	Page 113
What is the Importance of Childhood in the Novel?	Page 115
How does Dickens use Fred to explore aspects of Victorian society?	Page 117
What are Dickens's Messages in A Christmas Carol?	Page 119
How does Dickens Use Atmosphere and Setting?	Page 121
Your Turn: How is A Christmas Carol an Allegory or a Morality Play?	Page 125
Top Quotations	Page 127
Other Quotations Teachers Like	Page 132
Further Symbols	Page 134
Interpretations	Page 137
Key Vocabulary Explained	Page 140

Introduction

Many top performing schools don't teach **A Christmas Carol**, because they see the story as too simple.

Scrooge, the mean old miser and mankind-hating sinner is made to see the error of his misanthropic ways by four ghosts. First his dead partner Jacob Marley, and then the three Ghosts of Christmas, shape-shifting; fat, bearded and jolly; and the Grim-Reaper-Dementor type at the end, all combine to teach Scrooge the moral lessons which lead to his redemption.

The world turns from fog to sunshine, Scrooge turns from miserable miser to generous father figure, and Tiny Tim gets to live and hurray for Christmas, and hurrah for generosity and charity, what a wonderful world this could be. The End.

Where's the depth in that? So, we chuck in some Thomas Malthus (and get it wrong!) We stir in some gothic (it isn't really there though). We try to interpret the ghosts as dreams so we can sprinkle in a bit of Freud (ridiculous).

Well, this is a Mr Salles guide, so there will be depth everywhere. Strap into your sleigh and get ready for a whirlwind ride of top-grade ideas.

As usual, I write my guides with enough depth for you to get a grade 9 on whatever question you get in the exam. But you can skip all of this and still get a grade 9!

How? I've also included seven grade 9 essays which will cover any question likely to come up in the exam. You could simply skip to the essay section, and revise quickly and effectively there. I know. You're welcome.

Mr Salles

Swindon, Jewel of the M4

The Structure

The Five Act Structure of Tragedy
Dickens has chosen a five-act structure for his novel. This is actually typical of a Shakespearean tragedy. He makes his narrator refer to the ghost of Shakespeare's most famous tragedy, **Hamlet**, right at the start of the novel just to make sure we know what he is up to – playing with the idea of tragedy.

Five Stave Structure of a Carol to be Sung
However, because this is an inspirational story for Christmas, Dickens has the wonderful idea to call his chapters 'staves'. These are the five parts of a Christmas carol which his audience would sing in church. The intention is to be uplifting. He hints that, although Scrooge's story would have been a Shakespearean tragedy, Scrooge's transformation is an uplifting celebration of Christmas, celebrating the power of humanity and family.

The Ghost Story
Dickens is also playful in the way that he begins with a ghost story, not what we would expect of a Christmas experience. However, to a Victorian reader, winter ghost stories would be a tradition.

The famous first line, **"Marley was dead, to begin with"**, lets us know the supernatural genre we are about to enjoy. If I ask you to number how many ghosts appear in the story, you might guess three, the past, present and future spirits of Christmas, and you might add Jacob Marley. However, you would still be far short of the true total. This book is steeped in ghosts – not just Hamlet's father, but the dozens of businessman and government Scrooge is shown by Marley, and the child spirits of Ignorance and Want. The narrator also calls Scrooge and Marley **"two kindred spirits"**, a pun on the idea that they are both ghosts, not just Marley.

Structured for Performance
It's worth remembering how the book would have been read in Dickens' time. It would have been performed by a father or mother, or highly literate child, to the rest of the family during the long winter evenings. Families were trapped indoors, without electricity, radio, phones, Internet, television ... you get the idea. In Dickens' time, you made your own entertainment, and you learned to be pretty good at it. This novella is written as a performance. Dickens himself performed it dozens of times, to huge audiences, who were amazed at his ability to take on the different personalities of his characters. His next most popular performance was the violence, melodrama and pathos of **Oliver Twist** and the murder of Nancy.

In 1849 he began public readings of the story, which proved so successful he undertook 127 further performances until 1870, the year of his death.

The Happy Ending

The book is structured to provide entertaining horror and dread. Dickens wanted to deliver a slight chill in common with winter, rather than the gory shock fest we might be used to in the cinema.

Just as a five-act tragedy is propelled by the inevitability of fate, so the five-stave structure of a Carol demands to be completed, to come to a happy ending. Dickens' structure echoes this idea of inevitability when Marley tells Scrooge: **"You will be haunted… by three spirits"**.

The inevitability of the happy ending demanded by this structure has upset many critics. It has become fashionable to argue that Scrooge's conversion is not psychologically convincing. Obviously, because this is a Mr Salles guide, I will be arguing the opposite to the conventional view!

Edmund Wilson, an influential critic, said this:

> "Shall we ask what Scrooge would actually be like if we were to follow him beyond the frame of the story? Unquestionably, he would relapse, when the merriment was over - if not while it was still going on - into moroseness, vindictiveness, suspicion. He would, that is to say, reveal himself as the victim of a manic-depressive cycle, and a very uncomfortable person."

To which I say, "Humbug"!

The Choice of a Narrator Ghost

This type of objection to Scrooge's transformation is a strong reason why Dickens introduced a ghostly narrator, so we are forced to believe in the ending. Although the narrator helps establish the novel as a proper ghost story, and helps set a humorous tone (because it is a very jovial ghost) the ghost also has supernatural insight.

Consequently, at the end of Stave Five, it is not just Scrooge telling us that he is a changed man, or even Dickens himself. Instead, we are invited to believe it is an omniscient spirit who, as we have seen in the novel, lives outside of time and is therefore able to see the characters' fates. This invites us to believe that Scrooge's conversion is real. It isn't just a sentimental ending to please his sentimental readers at the most sentimental time of the year.

The Structural Symbolism of Death and Resurrection

Dickens also plays with the idea of resurrection and rebirth, because this is partly a Christian allegory. The Christian element of the story is downplayed. Dickens is much more interested in what we can do for our fellow man *now*, rather than waiting for salvation in heaven later. However, he needs to tap into his readers' Christian faith, using the imagery of resurrection after death. Consequently, Scrooge is introduced to us through descriptions that suggests he is already so frozen emotionally, that he appears dead. He appears little different from a corpse:

"External heat and cold had little influence on Scrooge. No warmth could warm, no wintry weather chill him."

The purpose of this description isn't just to reveal his complete lack of feeling for his fellow man, it is mainly to suggest a corpse that has no interest in heat or cold. This allows Dickens to prepare the transformation of rebirth in the final stave. In Stave Five, he repeatedly compares Scrooge to a baby:

"I'm quite a baby. Never mind. I don't care. I'd rather be a baby."

All Christian readers would recognise the parallel with the baby Jesus, whose birth they celebrate on Christmas Day.

The rebirth in the final stave is also the story of Tiny Tim, brought back from the dead, a death that could only be prevented by Scrooge's own rebirth:

"And to Tiny Tim, who did not die, he was a second father." Now we can see that Tiny Tim is the fulcrum around whom the whole story pivots. This is why Dickens gives him the final words of the novel, "God bless us, every one!"

This reminds all readers that the transformation is not just a feel-good Christmas tale, but a campaign for social justice. You'll see that Dickens demands us to make the lives of the poor, and poor children in particular, our top priority.

Ebenezer Scrooge

As you know, you get top grades by arguing different points of view. Scrooge is a character made for top grades.

Scrooge is a Two-Dimensional Character

We can argue that he is just a two-dimensional representation of what is wrong with Victorian society. Dickens believed that the Poor Laws were a criminal attack on the poor, with workhouses being little different to prison. Prison itself was also an attack on the family, who all became victims, because the whole family was imprisoned with the debtor, while their children were sent out to work.

Dickens himself was sent out to work in terrible conditions aged twelve, in Warren's Blacking factory, when his father and family were put into debtors' prison at Marshalsea. This is why Dickens gave Scrooge his famous lines in support of the workhouse and the prison.

Many critics point to the sudden turnaround in Scrooge, ridiculing his incredible transformation as psychologically unconvincing. You can't expect us to believe he would change a lifetime habit overnight, they say. The most famous of these is Edmund Wilson, whose essay **The Two Scrooges**, portrays Scrooge as a conflicted character, suggesting his is manic-depressive. He also argues that Dickens was also manic depressive.

Scrooge is a Psychologically Convincing Character

However, I'm also going to argue the opposite, and not just for higher grades. I'll try to show that actually Dickens had a deep understanding of what we now call psychology, and he would have called human nature. In particular, we will look at patterns of attachment, the idea that our earliest relationships have a long-lasting effect on our behaviour, even when we can no longer remember them.

Or, to borrow a phrase from William Wordsworth 40 years before Dickens, "the child is father to the man". Wordsworth himself stole the idea from Aristotle, writing around 350 BC, who is reported to have said "give me a child until he is seven and I will show you the man". The idea that our earliest experiences have far reaching consequences is powerful in Scrooge's story.

Dickens is fascinated by childhood in this novel, which is why we are going to meet Scrooge in order of age, rather than as he appears in the novel.

Stave Two

At School

"The spirit touched him on the arm, and pointed to his younger self, intent upon his reading."

Dickens could make Scrooge do anything – exploring the woods with his friends, stealing food from the kitchens, making friends with the caretaker's giant dog. He didn't, because he wasn't writing Harry Potter.

Making him a child who reads serves two purposes:

1. It explores Dickens' recurring passion about education and literacy as a way out of poverty, and a way to change society.

2. It explores Scrooge as a person with a creative imagination.

This creativity will explain why Scrooge can be such a hilarious villain, with some brilliant one liners. He teases Marley's ghost that he isn't real but caused by Scrooge's indegestion:
"There's more of gravy than of grave about you, whatever you are!"

His imagination and humour also accomplish two things:

1. We are not alienated by Scrooge, and we want him to transform, because we can sense a worthwhile person beneath his miserly personality.

2. He will have the imagination to see beyond his current self, and imagine what changing will look and feel like.

'Suddenly a man in foreign garments: wonderfully real and distinct to look at: stood outside the window, with an axe stuck in his belt, and leading by the bridle an ass laden with wood.

"Why, it's Ali Baba!" Scrooge exclaimed in ecstasy. "It's dear old honest Ali Baba! Yes, yes, I know. One Christmas time, when yonder solitary child was left here all alone, he did come, just like that. Poor boy!"'

Dickens makes Ali Baba an even more important piece of information than knowing Scrooge was abandoned at school by a cold father. He is "wonderfully real" again to emphasise two points:

1. The power of reading and literacy is truly transformative.

2. Scrooge's imagination is very highly developed, making his vision of his eventual transformation more plausible, or "real".

Dickens might also use Ali Baba because he comes from a deliberately non-Christian tradition – he features in **The Arabian Nights**, first translated into English in 1811 and then again in a new version in 1838. His intention is to show that Christmas is not so much a religious, Christian celebration, it is a celebration of man's humanity. It is the Christmas spirit, and the desire to make the world better.

Other critics use it to suggest that Scrooge is an outsider, unlike the rest of Christian society. As a miser, he forgets his Christian duty to help others.

But I like to argue that instead he is an insider – he reads the same books that Dickens' readers are reading because, Dickens is suggesting, he is just like them. The difference is that Scrooge is going to undergo a dramatic change. This becomes a challenge, where Dickens will symbolically ask his readers: will you change your views on the poor and choose to make a better future? Or will you simply discard this tale along with the Christmas wrapping paper?

Fan and Scrooge

"Father is so much kinder than he used to be, that home's like Heaven! He spoke so gently to me one dear night when I was going to bed, that I was not afraid to ask him once more if you might come home; and he said Yes, you should; and sent me in a coach to bring you. And you're to be a man!" said the child, opening her eyes, **"and are never to come back here; but first, we're to be together all the Christmas long, and have the merriest time in all the world."**

Fran is a two-dimensional character, in the sense that Dickens only introduces her for, you've guessed it, two reasons:

1. She can die and add a further level of grief and psychological explanation for Scrooge becoming a frozen, emotionless miser.

2. She can be the mother of Fred, who is the contrast to Scrooge. He is the mirror in which we can see Scrooge's future self. Fred is a wonderful human being, generous about Scrooge, even defending him to others, and insisting that there is still hope of changing him. Fred also shares 25% of Scrooge's genes, and so helps us see that Scrooge's transformation might actually be possible.

But the real point of this scene is what Fran reveals about Scrooge's father. Although he has created a "Heaven" at home, Scrooge is still not welcome. Fran has had to beg her father, repeatedly, over time, to let Scrooge live at home, even during the school holidays. His father has frightened her in the past, but now that he has transformed, she says **"I was not afraid to ask him once more."**

Well, there are so many top-grade ideas to explore here:

1. His father is still cold and indifferent, which is why he doesn't come with Fran to welcome Scrooge home.

2. Dickens portrays "heaven" as an illusion. Although a transformed father will no longer be deliberately cruel, he is still cold and distant. Perhaps Dickens sees God as failing to provide that warmth to the poor and suffering, so he asks his readers to do it instead.

3. Dickens might have been drawing a parallel to the greatest transformation of all – the God of the Old Testament to the God of the New Testament. The Old God drowned a whole planet apart from those on the Ark with Noah because he didn't like the way they behaved. The New God sacrificed his only son, allowing mankind to kill Jesus and then forgiving mankind, rather than taking terrible revenge. We could argue that Dickens wants to tap in to his readers' Christian faith, and use it to help them believe that great transformation is possible.

4. **"And you're to be a man"** emphasises Dickens' psychological point: bitter, old Scrooge is created by his pattern of attachment. His childhood has made the man.

Fezziwig's Apprentice (7 years in Dickens' time)

All apprenticeships lasted 7 years in Dickens' time. We might expect that 7 years of positive influence might change the negative influence of his early childhood. Dickens points out that this didn't happen.

"During the whole of this time Scrooge had acted like a man out of his wits. His heart and soul were in the scene, and with his former self. He corroborated everything, remembered everything, enjoyed everything, and underwent the strangest agitation."

Why does he make Scrooge relive every moment so passionately? One reason is that it foreshadows the transformation, where Scrooge can become much like his younger self – a better man.

But then we should ask, why did 7 years with such a wonderful role model as Fezziwig, where Scrooge seems truly "out of his wits" happy (without needing illegal substances), not have a profound effect on Scrooge as an adult? Or even a small influence? Why didn't those 7 years stop him becoming such a **"clutching, covetous old sinner"**?

It also makes us wonder this: if Scrooge was capable of so much celebration and enjoyment as a young man, who is also, we discover, in love, and about to be engaged, what changed? How did he ever transform into the "cold" miser of Stave One? How will that ever be psychologically convincing?

Critics might argue it is because Dickens isn't really interested in being psychologically convincing, he just wants to:

1. Set up Scrooge as a hero of the journey, on a quest to rediscover his former self and become a much better man.

2. More importantly, with Fezziwig, make a political and social point to employers, about their moral duty to improve the lives of their employees.

"It isn't that," said Scrooge, heated by the remark, and speaking unconsciously like his former, not his latter, self. "It isn't that, Spirit. He has the power to render us happy or unhappy; to make our service light or burdensome; a pleasure or a toil. Say that his power lies in words and looks; in things so slight and insignificant that it is impossible to add and count 'em up: what then? The happiness he gives, is quite as great as if it cost a fortune."

Here Dickens is preaching, through Scrooge's *epiphany* (a sudden and profound understanding – steal the word) that even our small kindnesses add up to a profound impact. All readers, he implies, can make a small change which will improve society and the lives of the poor.

Then Dickens makes totally clear, just in case any business owners are nodding off as their family read to them I suppose, that all businessmen should always think of their employees' wellbeing. Consequently, Scrooge immediately asks:

"… I should like to be able to say a word or two to my clerk just now."

Starting Out as a Money Lender

Once Scrooge has qualified at whatever business Fezziwig runs, he thinks, 'this is not me'. At some point he decides to become a money lender and replace the generous and fun-loving Fezziwig with the penny pinching, miserable Jacob Marley.

Before we get to Belle, it is worth asking why Dickens made Scrooge a money lender, rather than a factory owner, or a railway magnet, or an arms dealer. After all, this would give him many more employees whose lives he could change. Here are a few reasons:

1. Having only one employee makes a better case to the reader – every reader can imagine changing their responsibilities and behaviour to *one* poorer person. Few readers would have a large workforce, so they wouldn't identify with him.

2. But Dickins is also tapping in to his readers' Christian knowledge. Jesus attacked moneylenders because they took up business in the temple, the house of God and prayer.

"And Jesus went into the temple of God, and cast out all them that sold and bought in the temple, and overthrew the tables of the moneychangers, and the seats of them that sold doves." (Matthew 21, 12-13)

The money changers made a profit from the poor pilgrims who had to exchange Roman and Greek coins into Shekels, Jerusalem's currency. What was wrong with selling doves? They were the lowest form of sacrifice, (the Old Testament God was very keen on animal sacrifice) so again it was the poor who paid up money they couldn't really afford.

So, giving Scrooge this profession marks him out as un – Christian, as well as immoral. Even more significant for Dickens, though, is how he links exploiting the poor with being a bad Christian. He had to do this, because over 90% of his readers would have been Christian. Guilt is a wonderful way to influence them to look after the poor.

"Another idol has displaced me…A golden one…You fear the world too much…. All your other hopes have merged into the hope of being beyond the chance of its sordid reproach. I have seen your nobler aspirations fall off one by one, until the master passion, Gain, engrosses you."

Here we are with another goldmine of a quotation for those seeking top grades.

Dickens makes Belle characterise Scrooge not just as a miser, hoarding money. She uses religious imagery, so that Scrooge is worshipping an "idol" which is "golden", rather than just money.

The King James Bible is pretty obsessed with idols, and contains over 100 warnings against worshipping them, including one of the Ten Commandments. Dickens had in mind the link between idols and gold, which the Bible also condemns as un-Christian and heathen:

"The idols of the heathen are silver and gold." Psalms 135:15

Why was Scrooge Attracted to Belle?

Belle also offers us a psychological interpretation of Scrooge's motivation in worshipping wealth. She tells us they were "poor and content to be so". So, what changed wasn't a fear of poverty. It was a fear "of the world".

Belle says Scrooge fears "the chance of [the world's] sordid reproach". One meaning of this is that the poor are criticised by the wealthy and the middle class. To be poor is to be dirty, "sordid", and everyone treats you with disgust, and tells you to improve – this is what "reproach" means.

But look again. It is the world which is "sordid" here, not the poor. Specifically, the world's "reproach" is sordid.

Let's return to the lonely child in the classroom. Who has reproached him? His father. What form has that reproach taken? It is complete abandonment.

Think about this. Where is Scrooge's mother? Entirely absent because, we must infer, she is dead. Presumably after her death, Scrooge has been sent away to school by a father who dislikes him so much, that he won't let him come home, even at Christmas.

Then he is rescued by his sister, Fran. But his father still remains distant. How does the world "reproach" Scrooge? Well, first his mother dies – she metaphorically abandons him. Then Fran dies, and metaphorically abandons him again.

Then he falls in love with Belle. And she too abandons him, breaking off their engagement with **"I release you"**.

Pattern of Attachment Theory

So, what does pattern of attachment theory predict Scrooge will do? Incredibly, it says he will recreate the relationships of his youth, unconsciously, even if they damage him, because he won't be aware this is what he is doing.

He was abandoned by his mother and father, so he is naturally drawn to Belle, ***because*** she is likely to abandon him. You probably haven't spotted that she is much younger than him. Let me show you.

The ghost immediately takes Scrooge, and us, to visit Belle as a mother 7 years ago, at Christmas Eve. Scrooge watches Belle with her husband, their teenage daughter and their other children. The narrator decides that Scrooge is grieving because such a daughter could have been his and **"been a spring-time in the haggard winter of his life."**

This implies that Scrooge, only seven years after this scene, is already in the winter of his life. Every description of him confirms it elsewhere in the novel. He is already an old man.

So, Belle must have been much younger than Scrooge to have such a young family, and a baby, only 7 years ago. The average age of marriage for a woman in London of 1861 was around 24 and twenty years before that might have been 25. If Belle's daughter is a maximum of 19 years old, Belle is no older than 44.

Obviously, we can imagine exactly why Scrooge would be attracted to a younger woman. But we would be wrong. One reason to choose a much younger partner is to increase the likelihood that, as you age, she will leave you. This is an unconscious desire, caused by the pattern of abandonment his childhood-self experienced.

Next, his father was deeply critical of him, *so* he seeks a career which will make society deeply critical of him – he became a money lender.

He was alone as a child, and therefore chooses to have no friends as an adult, reproducing his early attachment. His only companion is Marley, an older version of himself, another money lender. But also, another one whose attachment is based on abandonment. Remember, Scrooge was his "sole mourner".

Why Does Scrooge Choose Marley?

Dickens deliberately links the two – the abandonment of Belle, and Scrooge's choice of Marley as a life partner, when the ghost takes him to see Belle and her happy family on Christmas Eve in the past when Marley is dying: **"His partner lies upon the point of death"**.

Remember, Scrooge and Marley are not just business partners, they live together in the same house. They are partners in the same way that a married couple are. When Marley dies, Scrooge inherits. It is also worth considering that he has also chosen Marley because he is older than Scrooge, and therefore likely to die first and metaphorically abandon him.

This would explain the otherwise strange details of Marley's appearance, **"Marley in his pigtail, usual waistcoat, tights and boots"**. The pigtail was no longer fashionable for a man in 1843, when the novel was published, and it would be obvious to Dickens' readers.

Although it is set earlier, at an unspecified date, the snowy Christmas scene would fit the late 1830s. The British Army introduced regulations to ban the pigtail in 1800, while the navy did the same in about 1820. Prior to that the pigtail had been the regulation cut. Marley, as an efficient miser, is simply maintaining the fashion of his youth, which is cheaper, and growing his hair long – again, cheaper to maintain.

But the main reason for this detail is to point out their difference in age. Dickens wants us to realise Marley was always likely to abandon Scrooge. We can choose to see this as very good business – Scrooge is likely to inherit.

Or we can add to this what we have seen of Scrooge's attachment, and realise that there is a psychological reason – Scrooge can't stop himself reproducing relationships which will lead to his being abandoned.

Seeing Belle and her family, and at the same time being reminded of the death of Marley is too much for Scrooge, and he physically attacks the ghost. This break in his personality reveals the strong psychological reason for Scrooge's change.

He realises he has thrown his life away by loving money. But more importantly, he realises that he has been the victim of attachment. He can see that all his relationship choices have been deliberate – he has chosen to be abandoned.

Stave One

Dickens reveals all those details in flashback of Stave Two. In Stave One he wants us to see Scrooge as a larger than life, theatrical figure. He is a villain, with brilliant dialogue. The intention is to both horrify his readers with such a dislikeable character, and entertain them with his villainy. He is also careful to make Scrooge very funny.

External heat and cold had little influence on Scrooge. No warmth could warm, not wintry weather chill him. No wind that blew was bitterer than he, no falling snow was more intent upon its purpose, no pelting rain less open to entreaty.

Dickens really wants us to enjoy the repetition, the anaphora of "no" and the alliteration of "wintry weather" and 'wind", emphasising Scrooge's cold personality. Then there is the driving rhythm of the plosive "p" in "purpose…pelting…open". This creates more than a memorable protagonist.

On a purely financial level, Dickens needs his readers to buy this very expensive book. What do they ask when they open the first page?

1. Will this book entertain me?
2. Will it entertain my family when I read it out loud?

Well, every technique I've focused on is about sound – its aural – and that's a yes from me, Charles, I'll buy this book to read to my family…

This extended metaphor, comparing Scrooge to terrible, winter weather, is carefully placed to prepare us for transformation. Just as snow melts and seasons pass, there is a hint that Scrooge himself might thaw.

Another hint that Scrooge will change is in the relish with which the narrator uses the past tense – the "Oh" and the "But" which begin the next quotation also hint at a turnaround in the present.

Oh! But he was a tight-fisted hand at the grindstone, Scrooge! a squeezing, wrenching, grasping, scraping, clutching, covetous old sinner! Hard and sharp as flint, from which no steel had ever struck out generous fire; secret, and self-contained, and solitary as an oyster.

Obviously, Dickens is still selling the performance value of his tale, and everything is rhythmic. The constant refrain of past participles, the hyperbolic list of verbs, the sibilance everywhere which suggests his evil nature, and the harsh consonance of C and K which suggests his cold cruelty. Say it out loud to get the flavour.

The effect is also deliberately comic. Imagine the final simile, "solitary as an …" and then the bizarre surprise of "oyster". First it makes us laugh. The sibilance also adds to the comic tone. Secondly, oysters are, to a Victorian audience, not solitary at all. If you've seen them on the rocks, they cluster in thousands. Simplyoysters.com tells us that:

> "In the 19th century, oysters were plentiful and cheap; and were sold on almost every street corner in London. Oysters were very popular with the lower class who used oysters as a substitute for expensive beef in stews and soups. One of the most popular Victorian dishes with the lower class was oyster pie."

On Victorian streets, they were also consumed in batches – by the bag, not alone. The image is doubly ridiculous to a Victorian, because oysters weren't solitary, but also, they were associated with poverty.

Now we can see how Dickens is playing with symbolism. Yes, an oyster potentially contains a pearl within, and yes, Scrooge's transformation is a metaphorical pearl. But does Dickens ever mention a pearl? No. Scrooge is not a pearl.

But "solitary" is comically wrong – so the symbolism is also that Scrooge's solitary state is also wrong, he will change.

If you want to go to town on this, you can also point out that "flint" is a tool associated with starting a fire – another thematic link which suggests his coldness might thaw.

Scrooge has Great Dialogue

Next Dickens emphasises Scrooge's wit. We are used to these in action movies, where the victim is killed while our hero delivers a brilliant one liner. Dickens invented the idea here:

If I could work my will," said Scrooge indignantly, "every idiot who goes about with 'Merry Christmas' on his lips, should be boiled with his own pudding, and buried with a stake of holly through his heart. He should!"

The reader is intended to partly agree with this, as anyone who has been to America will tell you. After hearing 'Have a nice day' twenty times on the same day you feel yourself, metaphorically of course, reaching for something sharp. The alliterative Bs also add to the enjoyment of this humour, again demanding to be performed out loud. The "stake of holly through the heart" is also a kind of genre joke – the vampire tale is exactly the kind of ghost story Dickens readers would expect at Christmas.

We could also argue that Scrooge's humour is also aimed at middle aged men, and older. It's worth pausing to consider why Dickens made Scrooge older. He would certainly have more time to improve the life of others if he were in his forties rather than his sixties. There are also endless fatal diseases to kill him off with in Stave Four so a younger Scrooge could still be faced with his own grave.

Now imagine you are Dickens, and you want to make a real difference to the treatment of the poor. You want people to reach deep into their own pockets, and give to charity. Who is your ideal reader? Who has amassed savings, and controls the families' financial affairs? Middle aged men. Scrooge is therefore an extreme version of this male reader who will want to hold on to their hard-earned money, and not give it away to help the "idle" poor.

Dickens consciously gives Scrooge dialogue to represent this view, that the poor deserve their poverty because they are workshy:

I don't make merry myself at Christmas and I can't afford to make idle people merry. I help to support the establishments I have mentioned—they cost enough; and those who are badly off must go there."

"Many can't go there; and many would rather die."

"If they would rather die," said Scrooge, "they had better do it, and decrease the surplus population. Besides—excuse me—I don't know that."

Thomas Malthus

Now you've probably been taught that Thomas Malthus, (1766 - 1834) a writer and economist, believed that the poor should receive no charity, because they consume too much food, have too many children, producing more poor people who demand even more food, and so really, the only sensible response is to, well, let's not beat about the bush, they are the idle poor after all...what was I saying, yes, the sensible thing is to let them die.

This is stretching it a little, as the Reverend Thomas Malthus was in fact a vicar, and unlikely to interpret Jesus's teaching as 'the meek shall inherit the grave' and 'the starving of the five thousand' and 'returning Lazarus to the dead'.

However, he did believe in population control, and thought it would be a really great idea if poor people stopped having children they couldn't afford to feed. We might think this is a little harsh, but give the guy a break – they didn't have modern agriculture, the poor were flocking into cities, cholera and other disease was spreading, the modern sewage system hadn't been invented, human excrement splattered the streets and filled up the Thames, every street was teeming with carts, waggons, carriages each and every one of which was pulled by a horse dropping a trail of manure.

Life expectancy in 1843 was still falling because of this, and would do so for another decade before the Victorians managed to add an extra 9 years of life expectancy by the time Queen Victoria died.

This is to point out:

a) Thomas Malthus wasn't a heartless lunatic when he wrote *'An Essay on the Principle of Population'*, published in 1798

b) He died 10 years before **A Christmas Carol** was written, so others in politics had altered his argument.

You should therefore write: 'Dickens discredits the Malthusian political view that the poor should be treated cruelly and denied too much assistance in order "to decrease the surplus population" through illness, disease, starvation and early death' but not 'Thomas Malthus believed that…'

Dickens' beef was not with Malthus, but with the politicians who used his thinking to justify mistreatment of the poor – as you will see in the section on Context, but you can easily quote **"are there no prisons"** and **"The Treadmill and the Poor Law are in full vigour, then?"** to show that Scrooge is simply voicing the political view of the time.

The important thing is that many of Dickens' readers would recognise their own thoughts in Scrooge's questions – they agreed with him!

Even Scrooge is shocked at his own one liner, **"If they would rather die," said Scrooge, "they had better do it, and decrease the surplus population."** He immediately qualifies this by adding carefully, **"Besides—excuse me—I don't know that."**

This is Dickens preparing for Scrooge's transformation and maintaining some likeability.

Stave Three: Preparing the Transformation

Stave Three, the middle of the novel, focuses brilliantly on the supporting characters. I say this, because they support the main argument Dickens is making through his novel, that we must all seek to make the lives of others better, in particular those we employ, and the poor.

He also uses Stave Three to mythologise Christmas, which was a stroke of marketing genius. How do you write a book which will keep selling? Make every reader associate it with an event which happens every year, for everyone. Christmas!

So, the most useful quotation to you, for any essay, is the one which proves Dickens' story is an allegory (that is, a story intended to educate).

"Spirit … I learnt a lesson which is working now. To-night, if you have aught to teach me, let me profit by it."

You can also point out that Scrooge deliberately uses a metaphor about "profit" to show that he is no longer thinking like a miser, in purely financial terms. Knowledge and education are "profit". Again, Dickens is preparing for the transformation.

Why do Dickens and Scrooge focus on Tiny Tim?

Well, it is fashionable to laugh and mock Dickens for his mawkish sentimentality. For much of my youth I couldn't bear to read him – all that endless description, and so many scenes concocted as tear-jerking moments. My favourite quotation about Dickens is from Oscar Wilde: ""One must have a heart of stone to read the death of little Nell without laughing." And I feel the same way about the death of Tiny Tim in this Stave.

But there are other ways of looking at this. Here's the first.

"Spirit," said Scrooge, with an interest he had never felt before, "tell me if Tiny Tim will live."

Ok, let's focus on his newly awakened interest here. It is highly probable that in all the years Bob Cratchit has worked for him, Scrooge has never known about Tiny Tim. Scrooge's irritation with Bob's Christmas spirit in Stave One was expressed: **"my clerk, with fifteen shillings a week, and a wife and family, talking about a merry Christmas. I'll retire to Bedlam."** Scrooge's logic would mention Tiny Tim as another reason not to be "merry", but he doesn't, because he doesn't know about Tiny Tim.

We can also infer that Scrooge identifies with Tiny Tim. Tiny Tim is going to face the ultimate abandonment – he is going to die. Scrooge also sees Bob as an incredibly loving father, who will also have to deal with this abandonment. Fatherhood is at the heart of this novel, as we saw with Scrooge's pattern of attachment – first the treatment by his own father, then the pain of seeing Belle and her family. Scrooge's change of personality starts with this ability to suddenly imagine what fatherhood might be like, and break the pattern of attachment.

Now he sees himself as responsible for Tiny Tim. If he can stop Bob being poor, Tiny Tim can have a better diet and a better chance of survival. This isn't just some theoretical link, but would have been incredibly visible at the time, with studies estimating anything from a third to a half of children in cities suffering from this form of malnutrition and lack of vitamin D.

With over a million chimneys darkening the sky, the lack of sunlight had to be countered with a good diet. The poor, of course, don't get a good diet. The same is true for rates of tuberculosis, a lung disease. And so Tiny Tim doesn't just die because Dickens is manipulating us with sentimentality. Tiny Tim dies because that's what you'd see on the streets near where you lived.

"If these shadows remain unaltered by the Future, none other of my race," returned the Ghost, "will find him here. What then? If he be like to die, he had better do it, and decrease the surplus population."

The ghost uses Scrooge's words against him. Dickens uses Scrooge's words against his readers, who probably came to the book with a moderated version of Scrooge's belief in the "idle" poor.

I think this is Scrooge's psychological turning point. Dickens, of course, lays on some more melodrama where Scrooge meets a trio of characters who have been stealing the sheet and curtains from his corpse's bed, and the shirt off his corpse's back. Then, the climax of the Stave comes with Scrooge on his knees, facing his own gravestone.

Scrooge has already made the connection of the death of Tiny Tim to his own death. Once the "spectre" has taken him to the Cratchit's to see how they cope without Tiny Tim, Scrooge asks:

"Spectre," said Scrooge, "something informs me that our parting moment is at hand. I know it, but I know not how. Tell me what man that was whom we saw lying dead?"

The death of Tiny Tim makes Scrooge understand his own death, which is why he asks this straight away. His **"I know not how"** shows us that this is a leap of intuition, an unconscious reasoning. This unconscious reasoning is replacing the damaging unconscious reasoning which was his pattern of attachment.

Scrooge also realises this is the final part of his lesson, so this must be his **"parting moment"** with the ghost.

This is important, because it tells us that his transformation is based on a changed understanding of his past behaviour. He isn't just changing because, you know, God is coming for his sinner's soul.

Instead, Scrooge realises that he doesn't just have to become a nice, generous person. He needs to get rid of the ghost of his father and his addiction to abandonment. He has to become a father figure to Tiny Tim.

He asks the ghost:

"Men's courses will foreshadow certain ends, to which, if persevered in, they must lead," said Scrooge. "But if the courses be departed from, the ends will change. Say it is thus with what you show me!"

Here Scrooge wants to know if he can change his fate. Dickens obviously phrases it with "Men's courses" rather than man to let the reader know he is talking about them, not just Scrooge.

But why didn't he write "Men's actions"? He has already used the word "action" twice in the novel, and "course" only once. It is because Scrooge has uncovered a deeper truth. It is not his actions that are the problem, it is what has motivated those actions. It is what has set the course. He realises that he has not been making those choices entirely out of free will, but actually by seeking to reproduce destructive patterns of attachment.

Stave Four: His Transformation

This knowledge helps Scrooge realise he has been, metaphorically speaking, frozen in time, wedded to the past. The line: **"I will live in the Past, the Present, and the Future"** only makes sense if we think of it in terms of breaking his pattern of attachment.

"I will honour Christmas in my heart, and try to keep it all the year. I will live in the Past, the Present, and the Future. The Spirits of all Three shall strive within me. I will not shut out the *lessons* that they teach. Oh, tell me I may sponge away the writing on this stone!"

Notice how he also talks about "lessons", more than one lesson.

Let's see what some experts have to say:

"He is shown the error of his ways by the ghosts that visit him and is redeemed by his own willingness to change. The moral message of the novella is that all human beings have the opportunity to behave in kinder ways towards each other." BBC Bitesize

"With *A Christmas Carol*, Dickens hopes to illustrate how self-serving, insensitive people can be converted into charitable, caring, and socially conscious members of society." SparkNotes

"Dickens creates a powerful positive message in this novella – everyone can change". York Notes

"Then, he realized something. You know what people like better than moralizing essays? Almost anything, including stories about ghosts. And Christmas. And happy endings.

"So, he whipped up a little haunted house number where a miserly old man who's given up on connecting with other humans gets a chance to turn his life around after a couple of ghosts show him the past, present, and potential future. Et voilà! *A Christmas Carol*. Jam-packed with a ton of Dickens's ideas about how we need to empathize with the poor and give as generously as possible to those worse off than us, this weird mashup of touchy-feely melodrama and straight-up horror quickly turned into the runaway bestseller we all know and love." Shmoop

You get the idea. Not many lessons, just a variation on the same lesson – be nice.

But that isn't what Scrooge is about. He isn't just choosing a different way of *behaving*. He is learning a different way of *being*. That can only happen when he understands the cause of his misanthropy. Just noticing the effect of disliking people is not enough to change him.

Take a look at the friends and adults that you know. Do they eat too much, drink too much, spend too much time on social media, take silly risks...and do they just not know? Of course not, they all know. Then can all see the effects. What they can't do is change. Because they don't know **why** they act the way they do.

Scrooge is different. He has finally understood the "why".

If you want to understand more about how your pattern of attachment is influencing your unconscious decision making, try Oliver James (2002; 2006): They F*** You Up: how to survive family life."

Stave Five

'I will live in the Past, the Present, and the Future!' Scrooge repeated, as he scrambled out of bed. 'The Spirits of all Three shall strive within me. Oh, Jacob Marley! Heaven, and the Christmas Time be praised for this! I say it on my knees, old Jacob, on my knees!'

It is interesting that Scrooge says this as soon as he wakes up, because it shows us Dickens wants us to think about this more than his change in being generous. "Scrooge repeated" because Dickens is helping us to rethink our own pasts. He needs us to remember not just the happy times of our own childhoods, but the relationships we had then and which we have unconsciously allowed to control our actions since.

Dickens and his Dad

Many critics point to Scrooge as representing the difficult relationship Dickens had with his own father, who couldn't afford to the upbringing of 10 children in Camden Town, and was sent to debtors' prison. Years later, when Dickens was successful, his father would write to Dicken's friends, asking for money. Scrooge's desire for money, they argue, springs from Dickens' father, John.

The poverty of the Cratchits, also in Camden Town, shows us that Dickens is very much replaying his own childhood in the novel, and dealing with his own past. This contextual knowledge is really useful to argue that Dickens doesn't just want us to give to the poor, he wants us to revisit our past selves to work out why we don't already do that.

Scrooge's attention to his "past" also reminds us of the importance of family. Generosity starts at home.

Dickens Wants Social Reform

'Now, I'll tell you what, my friend,' said Scrooge, 'I am not going to stand this sort of thing any longer...'and therefore I am about to raise your salary!'

Scrooge is now used to convey Dickens' social messages. His reference to Bob, and employee, as "my friend" tells all employers that they should think of their employees this way. They aren't literally friends, but they deserve the same consideration and kindness as you would give a friend.

Next, he points out that it is not enough just to be kind, you must also make a financial effort to help, "to raise...salary!" This is like a campaign for a minimum wage, which would have had a huge impact in Dickens time. Not just a better diet, lower infant mortality, but also an end to the punishing hours of child labour.

Social Reform as Rebirth

"I don't know what day of the month it is," said Scrooge. "I don't know how long I have been among the Spirits. I don't know anything. I'm quite a baby. Never mind. I don't care. I'd rather be a baby."

Next Dickens wants us to understand that this is a truly radical view. It is easy for his readers to simply gloss over his social message, and think only of giving to charity. Instead, Dickens gives Scrooge imagery which suggests we have to start from scratch, and rethink everything.

This is why Scrooge incongruously imagines himself as "a baby" and then tells us again, he'd "rather be a baby."

Christian Symbolism

This symbolism is also deeply Christian. Scrooge is waking up on Christmas day, the day Jesus was born. Dickens wants the reader to think of this particular baby. Even to an atheist, the question, 'what would Jesus do?' is a powerful question. You don't need a Christian faith to know that Jesus was a historical figure, who taught many of the lessons in the Gospels. It is worth pointing out that Dickens' faith was not strong.

He actually wrote his own version of the Gospels for his children in 1849, six years after writing this novel. It is really useful for us to know that he wrote it for performance, to be read out loud, because it emphasises the often-neglected aspect of *A Christmas Carol.*

Another similarity with *A Christmas Carol* is that Dickens' Gospel stories focus on Jesus as a teacher, (who just happens to perform miracles on the side) and it is tempting to understand Dickens' as a teacher. Scrooge becomes a teaching aid who, as we have seen, teaches us lessons about generosity, about social responsibility, about our duties as employers, and about examining our patterns of attachment which, like Marley's "chains" are binding us to a past we must escape.

"Scrooge was better than his word. He did it all, and infinitely more; and to Tiny Tim, who did not die, he was a second father. He became as good a friend, as good a master, and as good a man."

His final lesson reinforces all of these. The first three are emphasised in a triplet, reflecting Scrooge's desire to be a "good...friend...master...man."

The last one, the psychologically important one, which will allow Scrooge to change his behaviour, is to break the pattern of attachment. He rejects the lesson of abandonment taught to him by his father. He chooses to become "a second father" to Tiny Tim, so laying the ghost of his own father. And, we can imagine, this is also Dickens trying to lay to rest the all too present ghost of his own father.

Bob Cratchit

Bob Reveals Scrooge's Meanness and Cruelty

Yes, of course Dickens created Bob Cratchit to help his readers empathise with the harsh conditions of the poorer working classes. And yes, it is easy to dismiss him as very two dimensional, a construct invented to illustrate Dickens' social teaching, and to be the butt of many jokes.

This is definitely how he is introduced to us at first:

Scrooge had a very small fire, but his clerk's fire was so very much smaller, that it looked like one coal. But he couldn't replenish it, for Scrooge kept the coal-box in his own room; and so surely as the clerk came in with the shovel, the master predicted that it would be necessary for them to part. Wherefore the clerk put on his white comforter, and tried to warm himself at the candle….

We first find out about Bob from Scrooge's point of view, which is why we are first told that he is a "clerk", and we are not introduced to his name because, it seems, Scrooge doesn't care what his name is.

We can also see that he is afraid of Scrooge, and makes do **"with what looked like one"** piece of coal to keep warm by, without daring to ask for more. He knows that Scrooge would sack him just for requesting more coal. Scrooge describes this likely sacking totally unemotionally: **"the master predicted that it would be necessary for them to part".** Dickens wants to show how Bob is the victim of a harsh but, at this stage, typical employer.

Dickens symbolically dresses him with a **"white comforter"** in order to symbolise his innocence and purity. We are made to feel sympathetic because one candle seems to give more heat than the coal fire! And despite the darkness of winter, he has to see with the light on only one candle.

Why Do We Need to Know Bob's Salary?

Scrooge also makes fun of Bob for feeling positive in these terrible conditions:

He stopped at the outer door to bestow the greetings of the season on the clerk, who, cold as he was, was warmer than Scrooge, for he returned them cordially. "There's another fellow," mustered Scrooge, who overheard him; "my clerk, with fifteen shillings a week, and a wife and family, talking about a merry Christmas. I'll retire to Bedlam."

Although Scrooge is an exaggerated form of the heartless Victorian employer, Bob is slightly closer to reality. This is why Dickens is very explicit about how much Bob is paid, "fifteen shillings" a week.

Firstly, we can see that Scrooge knows this is not enough to support a wife and family, because he tells himself such a salary should prevent Bob from feeling any kind of Christmas spirit. In fact, this is so little, that Scrooge imagines Bob is insane. This is why he imagines retiring to the country's most famous mental hospital, "**Bedlam**", suggesting that Bob's extreme sort of madness would prepare Scrooge for the much milder madness he would find there.

Why Do We Need to Know the Cost of the Novel?

The other purpose of the 15 shillings is to ask his readers to compare the cost of the novel to what a poor employee might be earning – it was 5 shillings, virtually a third of Bob's wage. 20 shillings made a pound! The reader would be stunned at how much they have paid for an entertainment, compared to how much a worker might have to spend on their whole family for the entire week.

This is deliberate. Dickens normally sold his books much cheaper, but he made sure this was a luxury edition. To put that into context, he sued a rival publisher who plagiarised the book and sold it for 1 penny – one sixtieth of the price of his book! So, Dickens could have made a huge profit selling it much cheaper – desperate readers were out there. But he didn't, because wealthy people don't shop in Aldi and Lidl. They shop at Waitrose. He needed wealthy readers, because they are the ones who could make a difference to wages and the law.

Bob is Contrasted with Scrooge

Finally, Dickens shows how much better Bob is than his employer, still able to be cheerful despite his frozen state. Here Dickens makes the point that workers are possibly better human beings than their entitled employers. This contrast with Scrooge invites the reader to ask if they should be more like Bob.

Bob and the Mythology of Christmas

Bob is also used to mythologise Christmas. Remember, writing a novel about Christmas was unique. Dickens pretty much made up a new genre. Better than that, he knew he could repeat this genre, because Christmas just keeps on coming every year. It was marketing genius.

So, he made Bob excited about Christmas. Really excited!

The office was closed in a twinkling, and the clerk, with the long ends of his white comforter dangling below his waist (for he boasted no great-coat), went down a slide on Cornhill, at the end of a lane of boys, twenty times, in honour of its being Christmas Eve, and then ran home to Camden Town as hard as he could pelt, to play at Blindman's buff.

Bob is incredibly playful and childlike. He joins in with a "**lane of boys**" flinging himself down a slide to show that he has retained a zest for life, which contrasts with Scrooge's loss of that zest. He goes down the slide "twenty times" to illustrate his tremendous energy, despite his poverty, and despite the cold conditions he works in.

However, the detail that he does not own a "great-coat", but only a "white comforter", (a scarf) suggests that all this joyous physical activity is also necessary to keep warm. This is a second reason why Bob chooses to run all the way home to "**Camden Town**" as fast **"as he could pelt"**, which is a journey of over three miles as the crow flies – much longer following the layout of streets. Dickens wants his readers to imagine the energy it would take to run home for three miles in the snow.

This is another way that Dickens shows that Christmas has a special magic. He returns home desperate to play "**Blindman's buff**" with his family, so he runs at full "**pelt**". Dickens probably had in mind the homonym, 'pelt' meaning animal coat – he subtly reminds us that Bob has no coat. This playfulness conveys his inner joy, celebration of life, and celebration of Christmas. Again, it helps to provide a contrast to the despicable Scrooge.

Dickens has not asked for our sympathy. He allows his readers to make the contrast with their own lives, and then question how typical Bob's circumstances are of the poor working classes. He is gentle in this approach, using comedy to bring his readers along with him, leading them towards his social themes.

Dickens Laughs at the Working Classes (as his Wealthy Readers Will)

Oh, a wonderful pudding! Bob Cratchit said, and calmly too, that he regarded it as the greatest success achieved by Mrs. Cratchit since their marriage. Mrs. Cratchit said that now the weight was off her mind, she would confess she had had her doubts about the quantity of flour. Everybody had something to say about it, but nobody said or thought it was at all a small pudding for a large family. It would have been flat heresy to do so. Any Cratchit would have blushed to hint at such a thing.

Although Dickens wants us to connect emotionally with his working-class characters, he's also very happy for us to laugh at them. The idea that this pudding is the greatest success Mrs Cratchit has had "**since their marriage**" is delightfully ridiculous. It's also a little bit cruel to all the assembled children, whose births clearly take second place.

In this way Dickens also makes fun of his own celebration and mythologizing of the Christmas feast for all his readers. By suggesting the feast is even more important than family, he's really telling his readers that their time together as a family is the most precious gift of Christmas.

He also uses Bob's delight at the Christmas pudding to show how necessary it is for the poor to delight in even the smallest luxuries. The masterful understatement which finishes the paragraph reveals that the pudding is very tiny indeed. The contrast of "**small pudding**" and "**large family**" also emphasises their poverty. The family reaction, not to even "hint" at its small size, is also comic, and poignant. Again, though, Dickens has observed a psychological truth. People who have limited choices have the ability to artificially create happiness – the term is 'synthetic happiness', and is a very successful coping mechanism.

Synthetic Happiness

We will notice this synthetic happiness again when Tiny Tim dies, and Bob calls himself "happy". The act of pretending to be happy actually does make us happy, which is a useful life skill.

The idea that they would listen to "**the pudding singing in the copper**" is a wonderful personification of their joy. The pudding is in fact being steamed, so the noise would be the sound of escaping steam. A further point all Dickensian readers would know is that the pudding was popular with the poor because they could not afford an oven – Christmas puddings do not need an oven.

This "pudding" soon gets followed by "**a shovel full of chestnuts**" on the fire. Although this sounds like a plentiful alternative, the "shovel" does not imply an abundant stock. It is simply the tool used to place coals on the fire. They may well just be a Christmas treat. Readers, on the other hand, would find street sellers selling cooked chestnuts at virtually every corner during the winter and could happily eat them daily. Here again Dickens uses the Cratchits to prompt his readers to contrast their fortunes with Bob's.

Bob's Salary and Scrooge the Employer

Though they have little food, Bob is astonishingly able to see the best in Scrooge. **"Mr. Scrooge!" said Bob; "I'll give you Mr. Scrooge, the Founder of the Feast!"**

We can choose to see this as stretching credulity, especially as Mrs Cratchit protests, **"I'd give him a piece of my mind to feast upon"**. We can argue Bob is a two-dimensional character here. Or, we can think of the economics of the situation.

Even though Scrooge is a terrible employer, he has still given Cratchit a job. We find out in a moment that Bob's eldest son Peter might get a job for five shillings and sixpence a week, which is just over a third of what Cratchit himself is paid. Dickens points out the exact figures to us in pounds and pence, because he wants his readers to focus on the specifics of poverty.

Although Scrooge is a horrible miser, these figures reveal that the wages he pays are actually in line with the rest of society. Consequently, they are in line with what Scrooge's readers, those who are employers, are likely to be paying their own staff. We can therefore see Bob's appreciation of Scrooge as genuine in his mind, though ironic in Dickens' mind.

It is very easy for a modern reader to see the novel as an amusing and inspirational tale urging us all to spread Christmas cheer and give liberally to charity. That really diminishes what Dickens wants to achieve. He wants his readers to realise that being polite and jovial, and wishing everyone a Merry Christmas, and even giving their staff a party on Christmas Eve, is nowhere near as beneficial as actually paying them a fair wage.

It also helps if we don't see Bob as some sort of jovial simpleton, a simple victim of Scrooge's cruelty. Instead, he stays with Scrooge because his rate of pay compares well to any other job he might get. Why does Dickens do this? To show that society is no better than a "clutching, covetous old sinner!"

Bob and Tiny Tim

It would be easy to dismiss his relationship with Tiny Tim as an overly emotional tug at the heartstrings.

He sat very close to his father's side, upon his little stool. Bob held his withered little hand in his, as if he loved the child, and wished to keep him by his side and dreaded that he might be taken from him.

Bob completely understands that Tiny Tim is likely to die, and this knowledge is so deeply ingrained that he has a physical reaction to it. He holds onto his son's hand, sits as close to him as possible, as though he can physically hold on when death comes to take Tiny Tim away.

Life Expectancy: Infant Mortality in 1843

It would be easy to dismiss this imagery as purely sentimental, until we find out how common infant mortality was. 2007 research provides horrifying figures of infant mortality in London from 1825 to 1850: 30% of children died before the age of 6. Amazingly, the rate was similar for wealthy families. Bob's fear of Tiny Tim dying is a fear all Dickens' readers would have felt about their own families. It is impossible for us to imagine this with our enormous gap in time since 1843. As I write, the peak of the Coronavirus pandemic in the UK was April 2020, where we recorded 53.4 deaths per 100,000 people. Assuming children under 6 formed only 5/70ths of the population in 1843, this would give us 2381 deaths per 100,000, 45 times worse than the pandemic which closed down the UK for months. Imagine the underlying fear hidden beneath that normal statistic.

Dickens had spent the year 1843 touring factories and tin mines that employed children. He was horrified by their working conditions. He desperately wanted stop this. But instead of writing the political pamphlet that he wanted to write, he created characters who he thought might have a much greater impact on the behaviour of readers. This is why Bob can't just be a sentimental figure, but needs to be a character who deals with real issues in Victorian society.

The other reason for Bob's portrayal as a loving father is to provide a contrast to Scrooge's upbringing. Dickens obviously wants us to sympathise more with Scrooge than we did in Stave One. This moment also contributes to Scrooge's psychological understanding about the damaged caused to him by his past and by his relationship with his father. Giving Scrooge a lesson in fatherhood helps him to become "a second father" to Tiny Tim in the transformation of Stave Five.

Bob and the Death of Tiny Tim

Many readers are also very critical of the way Dickens shows Bob using Tiny Tim's death. When I first read it, I found it both implausible and totally lacking in human feeling:

But however and wherever we part from one another, I am sure we shall none of us forget poor Tiny Tim—shall we—or this first parting that there was among us? … And I know… I know my dears, that when we recollect how patient and how mild he was; although he was a little, little child, we shall not quarrel easily among ourselves and forget poor Tiny Tim in doing it.

"No, never, father!" they all cried again.

"I am very happy," said little Bob, "I am very happy!"

It's very difficult to read this scene as a modern reader. Bob seems to be using the death of his son as a way to teach his other children to stop quarrelling. This seems callous and unfeeling, as though he never really loved Tiny Tim at all.

However, this is also a profound meditation on life. What do you do in the face of personal tragedy, such as the death of someone very close to you? First, you celebrate what you loved about that person, in this case how "patient" and "mild" Tiny Tim was, despite his life of suffering and disability. Tiny Tim would also have lived with the knowledge that he had a high chance of dying too.

Next you try to make that person's life important to your future, and ask what lesson they taught you. Here, Tiny Tim's lesson is to teach patience and stoicism to his family. If terrible things keep happening to you, a mechanism which helps you carry on despite life's unfairness is very useful.

When Bob repeats he is "very happy", it is because he has learned a valuable lesson from his son, and this lesson has been passed on to the whole family. The alternative is to curse an uncaring God who would allow hunger, illness, and early death. Instead, by looking to the lessons Tiny Tim's death and life might teach the whole family, Bob is trying to make sense of a world in a way that gives his whole family hope. And from hope, comes happiness.

You might also have missed that he is preparing the family for further tragedy, and the inevitability of more deaths, emphasising that this is only the first such death: **"this *first* parting that there was among us"**.

Far from being a two-dimensional, unrealistic portrayal, Dickens uses Bob to help his readers deal with their own grief. Then he wants them to reach out, and help the poor who, his readers would expect, had more tragedies in their lives to grieve over.

Bob at the End of the Novel

At the end of the novel, Dickens does use Bob as a comic foil to Scrooge's transformation. Bob arrives "eighteen minutes and a half" late on Boxing Day, having celebrated Christmas fully, with the gift of the mysterious and gigantic turkey, which he doesn't know came from Scrooge.

"Now, I'll tell you what, my friend," said Scrooge, "I am not going to stand this sort of thing any longer. And therefore," he continued, leaping from his stool, and giving Bob such a dig in the waistcoat that he staggered back into the Tank again; "and therefore I am about to raise your salary!"

Bob trembled, and got a little nearer to the ruler. He had a momentary idea of knocking Scrooge down with it, holding him, and calling to the people in the court for help and a strait-waistcoat.

This lateness is not the Bob we would expect. It is as though having a full stomach has changed his personality. Perhaps this is Dickens' way of pointing out his readers' prejudice that, if they give their workers more, their workers will take advantage of them.

For this reason, he immediately makes Scrooge offer Bob a pay rise. He's pointing out to his readers that their fear of the working class is inhumane. He also does this very comically by describing Bob's reaction. Bob sees Scrooge's generosity as a sign of madness. He moves "nearer" to his "ruler" in order to defend himself.

It's interesting that he "trembled" at this, because in his imagination it's clear that he would easily be able to restrain Scrooge. His fear, although very funny, hides a serious point. If Scrooge does show signs of mental illness, Cratchit will lose his job because Scrooge will no longer be able to run his business.

It also suggests to us that the pattern of Bob's, and therefore working class, experience is that wonderful good fortune is rare, and usually followed by catastrophe. The joy of yesterday's turkey, a Christmas miracle, must surely be followed by calamity: an insane employer, the loss of a job, further poverty, panic, desperation.

Because it is Christmas, and because Scrooge has transformed, Dickens doesn't take us down that path of an unhappy ending. But he wants his readers to know it is there, and that millions of poor people walk it every day.

Fred

Fred is not just Scrooge's nephew. He is a painful reminder of Fan's death. Fred is introduced to be both Scrooge's his antithesis (his opposite) and a role model for how he can change in the future.

The Importance of Christmas

Dickens makes him praise Christmas:

"Though it has never put a scrap of gold or silver in my pocket, I believe that it has done me good, and will do me good; and I say, God bless it!"

Dickens uses this to teach Scrooge the lesson that life is much, much more than accumulating wealth. More than that, Fred shows that we can't measure the worth of the really valuable things in life through money.

The idea of Fred as Scrooge's opposite is deliberately highlighted through contrast. Scrooge tells Fred **"You're poor enough"**, implying that only wealth can bring happiness. Fred replies, **"You're rich enough"**, implying that holding on to your wealth, without spending it on others, will bring no happiness.

For Fred, this is joy in the family. This is a lesson Scrooge will learn when he visits Fred's family with the ghost of Christmas Present. It is worth pausing to notice that Dickens could have called the ghost 'Christmas Now' or 'Christmas Day' or simply 'Christmas', but these lack the secondary meaning of 'Present'. This ghost gives Scrooge his family back, through Fred, and this gift of course is the "present".

The Importance of Family

At the beginning the idea of family terrifies Scrooge. Dickens makes that clear to us when Scrooge refuses to say why he won't visit Fred for dinner on Christmas day. Instead, he asks Fred:

"Why did you get married?" said Scrooge.

"Because I fell in love."

"Because you fell in love!" growled Scrooge, as if that were the only one thing in the world more ridiculous than a merry Christmas. "Good afternoon!"

This helps us understand that Scrooge is afraid of feeling "love", having been rejected by Belle. This also implies that the only reason to marry is for financial gain. This is why Belle rejected Scrooge. She realised he would bitterly resent her because he was marrying her without a dowry, or with a very small one:

"Our contract is an old one. It was made when we were both poor and content to be so, until, in good season, we could improve our worldly fortune by our patient industry."

Fred has also married for love, without a good dowry, or **"contract"**. On the one hand he is the antithesis of Scrooge. But on the other hand, Scrooge was much like Fred when young. This implies there is hope for him to become like Fred again, and value love. And we should also notice that perhaps Scrooge believes in love more than money – he hasn't married for money, despite Belle's prediction.

Fred and Scrooge's Attachment to Abandonment

As you will know from my Scrooge analysis, his pattern of attachment makes him both fear and seek out this abandonment.

We also get a sense that Scrooge can't face Fred because he reminds Scrooge of his dead sister, Fan. First his mother, and then his sister abandoned him by dying. The Ghost tiptoes around the subject because he might realise it is so painful.

Have Fred's Siblings Died?

We get a sense of this in his tentative language, noting Fan "**had, as I think, children**". This diplomacy also hints at a tragic end to the other children. Only Fred appears to be alive. At his Christmas party we meet his wife and friends, but no siblings. This is also an important detail to help us understand the impact of Tiny Tim's death on Scrooge, because it shows that childhood death is not just a melodramatic addition to the novel, it is a fair reflection of the infant mortality statistics of the time.

We can also sense Scrooge's fear of kindness as a physical weakness. So, the ghost's description of Fan as **"Always a delicate creature, whom a breath might have withered," said the Ghost. "But she had a large heart!"** suggests her kindness, symbolised by the "large heart" was too much for her frail body to bear.

We can also imagine that Scrooge is protecting himself against further loss. It is his pattern of attachment to expect abandonment. Abandoning Fred first will make this less painful for Scrooge, because life has taught him that everyone he loves is taken away from him by death.

Fred Enjoys Teasing Scrooge

Fred isn't just warm hearted and generous. At least a small part of his determination to wish Scrooge a merry Christmas is caused by Scrooge's misanthropic reaction: he simply enjoys provoking Scrooge into outrageous comments:

"He has given us plenty of merriment, I am sure," said Fred, "and it would be ungrateful not to drink his health. Here is a glass of mulled wine ready to our hand at the moment, and I say, 'Uncle Scrooge'!... A Merry Christmas and a Happy New Year to the old man, whatever he is!"

Proposing a toast to his friends in this way suggests he regularly shares stories of Scrooge's cantankerous personality in order to make his wife and friends laugh. Obviously, he isn't just making fun of Scrooge – he does genuinely return every year to try to improve Scrooge's view of humanity, of his employee Bob, and his own ability to enjoy his wealth and life.

Fred also realises that Scrooge's attempts to protect himself from feelings of loss actually damage him, so that he pities Scrooge: **"I am sorry for [Scrooge]. I couldn't be angry with him if I tried. Who suffers by his ill whims? Himself always."** Fred realizes, far earlier than Ebenezer Scrooge does, that being stingy and cruel causes more suffering to the miser than to those around him. Indeed, in the beginning of the novella, Scrooge is lonely, cold, poorly fed, and stingy with himself. He is clearly unhappy in his life while those around him, like Fred and Bob Cratchit, are still able to find happiness, love, and joy.

Fred and Victorian Attitudes to Inheritance

Dickens also needs us to know that Fred is not financially motivated. He is not looking for any part of Scrooge's wealth.

"I want nothing from you; I ask nothing of you; why cannot we be friends? . . . But I have made the trial in homage to Christmas, and I'll keep my Christmas humour to the last. So, a Merry Christmas, uncle!"

Dickens wants his readers to reject the idea of personal fortune and the desire for wealth. This is why he makes Fred so clear in his statement to Scrooge. Next, he uses Fred to repeat **'Christmas'** three times, and let his readers know that Fred is his mouthpiece, celebrating the power of Christmas. Fred is a proxy for Dickens' views.

Dickens' books are obsessed with inheritance – ***Great Expectations*** being the most famous. To be truly free, in Dickens' moral universe, a man needs to live an independent life, without waiting to inherit wealth from others. This is both a personal badge of honour – Dickens was entirely a self-made man – but also social criticism. The expansion of the British Empire meant that the aristocracy and the rich business owners had vast fortunes to hand on to their relatives, so that a gentleman might never work at all. Dickens didn't respect them.

Dickens delighted in criticising characters who were obsessed with inheritance and the way they try to manipulate each other. It is important that we realise Fred has no interest in inheriting Scrooge's fortune (though as his only relative it is perhaps inevitable).

"His wealth is of no use to him. He don't do any good with it. He don't make himself comfortable with it. He hasn't the satisfaction of thinking—ha, ha, ha!—that he is ever going to benefit US with it."

Fred and the Role of Employers

Instead he wants Scrooge to experience the pleasure of helping others.

Fred's main concern is not **"US"**, but Bob: **"If it only puts him in the vein to leave his poor clerk fifty pounds, that's something; and I think I shook him yesterday."** Here Dickens wants his readers not just to focus on their own families, but on the people they employ. Many of his readers would run small businesses, like Scrooge. Even more, though, would have domestic servants, once family income rose above £150 per year. Scrooge, of course, is too much of a miser to employ anyone to look after his home, but the opposite would be true of his readers.

A huge number of them would therefore be employers. In the 1891 census, 1.3 million women were listed as domestic servants in Britain.

Because Dickens uses Fred to represent the Christmas spirit, he uses a circular structure to make Scrooge more like him at the end. The narrator therefore focuses on Fred's laugh: **'If you should happen, by any unlikely chance, to know a man more blest in a laugh than Scrooge's nephew, all I can say is, I should like to know him too. Introduce him to me, and I'll cultivate his acquaintance.'**

The fist description of Scrooge in Stave Five sees him **"laughing and crying in the same breath"**. The Stave also ends with a focus on Scrooge's laughter: **"His own heart laughed: and that was quite enough for him."** This brings us full circle to Fred so that Scrooge has become like Fred.

Fred is an optimist, who implausibly believes he has had an impact on Scrooge. This is why his family laugh at him for saying **"I think I shook him yesterday"**.

"It was their turn to laugh now at the notion of his shaking Scrooge. But being thoroughly good-natured, and not much caring what they laughed at, so that they laughed at any rate, he encouraged them in their merriment, and passed the bottle joyously."

However, we might also argue that Fred is right – he has begun the process which Marley has continued, and which the spirits will finish. Through Fred, Dickens introduces the idea that a reader can influence the behaviour and generosity of their wider family.

This description of Fred being teased by his family, and shrugging off their laughter is also vital to Dickens' circular structure. At the end of Stave Five, Scrooge also shrugs off being laughed at: **"Some people laughed to see the alteration in him, but he let them laugh, and little heeded them; for he was wise"**.

Scrooge has learned from his nephew to become, not just a better man, but a joyful man.

Jacob Marley

Old Marley was as dead as a door-nail.

Our narrator, also a ghost, uses Marley to get us to think about death. A "doornail", he suggests, is not "particularly dead". This provides a deliberately comic tone to the beginning of his ghost story. But it also asks us to think of death as something useful for the living, as a doornail is - it is a stud added to strengthen the door.

Marley's death is going to be similarly useful for Scrooge, and also for Dickens. He will use Marley's death to try to make life better for everyone else, if only they will learn the moral lessons of the book.

Marley and the Symbolism of Doors

You might also notice that Marley is obsessed with doors. This is why he first appears in a door, replacing the door knocker: **"not a knocker, but Marley's face."** Next, he enters **"through the heavy door"** which Scrooge had just double locked.

Perhaps we might argue that this symbolism is to remind his readers that death is coming for them - it can't be locked out. But also, that every door can be opened, as a doorway to a better future, or becoming a better human being.

Because Marley has no future, perhaps, he exits via the window, **"floated out upon the bleak, dark night."** Certainly, the "bleak, dark" adjectives suggest Marley has little hope of a better future. However, he does hint that his "procurement" of a second chance for Scrooge might help him reduce his time in the purgatory of wandering the earth, unable to help people.

This is contrasted with Scrooge, who Dickens moves towards the door, **"It was double-locked, as he had locked it with his own hands, and the bolts were undisturbed. He tried to say "Humbug!" but stopped at the first syllable."**

Dickens shows us that Scrooge has trapped himself in his own life, "as he had locked it with his own hands". Marley appears in the door to symbolically suggest that Scrooge should be metaphorically open, rather than locked.

What Sort of Partner is Marley

Scrooge knew he was dead? Of course he did. How could it be otherwise? Scrooge and he were partners for I don't know how many years. Scrooge was his sole executioner, his sole administrator, his sole assign, his sole residuary legatee, his sole friend, and sole mourner.

Jacob is Scrooge's surrogate wife. Dickens could have set Scrooge up to be trading on his own, or running a much larger business, with more employees than Bob Cratchit. He could have found a different ghost to warn him - for example the ghost of his father. Instead, Dickens chooses a ghost who has been with Scrooge **"for I don't know how many years"**, like a marriage.

Dickens also uses Marley playfully. The repetition of "sole" emphasises the link between Scrooge's 'soul' and the danger of not becoming a better man.

Dickens also emphasises Scrooge's good nature at the end, where he is Marley's **"sole friend, and sole mourner"**. This homophone (a word which has the same sound as another word) is important, because it hints that Scrooge can be saved and redeemed.

Marley in his pig-tail, usual waistcoat, tights, and boots; the tassels on the latter bristling like his pig-tail, and his coat-skirts, and the hair upon his head.

Dickens also makes Marley a comic and ridiculous ghost. Although he died only seven years ago, his 'pig-tail' and 'tights' were fashionable, from the reader's perspective, around forty years ago. These details also show that, like Scrooge, Marley was a miser and did not waste money on clothes. But Dickens doesn't make fun of Scrooge's fashion this way, which might mean that Scrooge himself was less of a miser than his partner. Perhaps it suggests there is more hope that Scrooge can change in his lifetime, in contrast to Marley who is only able to try to change too late - once he is dead. This is an important detail when you have to argue whether Scrooge's Stave Five conversion is plausible.

How is Marley Influenced by Dickens' Father?

The chain he drew was clasped about his middle. It was long and wound about him like a tail; and it was made (for Scrooge observed it closely) of cash-boxes, keys, padlocks, ledgers, deeds, and heavy purses wrought in steel. His body was transparent; so that Scrooge, observing him, and looking through his waistcoat, could see the two buttons on his coat behind.

It is easy to see, in this description of Marley's "chain" and the links made of "cash-boxes" and "heavy purses", that Dickens is revisiting his father's time in debtor's prison. His father was imprisoned for debt, and Dickens has reversed this. Marley's eternal prison is an obsession with wealth. But it probably goes deeper than that. Scrooge and Marley are money lenders, which means their wealth depends on other people's debt. They are, in some way, a cause of his father's poverty, imprisonment and Dickens' childhood unhappiness. The chain symbolises how Marley is being punished for his business and exploitation of the poor, which we can see Dickens takes personally.

How Dickens Creates Marley for Performance

Dickens also wants the descriptions to be incredibly vivid. They are visually detailed, so that Scrooge even notices the "two buttons" through Marley's "transparent" body. But they are also aural: the alliterative Cs of **"chain...clasped...like...cash...keys...padlocks"** mimic the clinking sound of the chain. Part of Dickens' skill, remember, is to craft a story to be read out loud and performed, to fit with the tradition of telling ghost stories around the fire during the winter.

"I wear the chain *I forged in life*," replied the Ghost. "I made it link by link, *and yard by yard*; I girded it on of my own free will, *and of my own free will I wore it*. Is its pattern strange to you?"

Marley's speech here is incredibly rhythmic, like a well-rehearsed church sermon. Notice how it is constructed out of evenly balanced phrases which delight in repetition, as I show with the italics. This allusion to the rhythms of a sermon is picked up on in the subject matter, the focus on "free will". The idea of "free will" is an important Christian idea, which Christians rely on to explain the extraordinary amount of evil in the world.

The Story of Free Will

If you come back with me to the first book of the Bible, Genesis, you may remember that God allowed Adam and Eve to behave exactly as they wished in The Garden of Eden.

In a way the God of the Old Testament sets Adam and Eve, and therefore mankind, to fail. He plants two special trees in The Garden of Eden: one is "The Tree of Life". If Adam and Eve eat its fruit, they will live forever. God plays a kind of inverse Russian Roulette, where Adam and Eve might by chance eat its fruit and, instead of dying, become immortal.

However, God warns them about the second tree: "But of the tree of the knowledge of good and evil, thou shalt not eat of it: for in the day that thou eatest thereof thou shalt surely die."

In this way, God sets up an experiment in free will. He does this to allow man to choose good over evil.

Whether Adam and Eve can even understand what "die" means is questionable. For example, until they eat from this tree, they don't even know what "naked" means, though they have always been naked. It is simply knowledge they don't have.

Well, Eve is the first to fail this test, and eat the fruit, and then Adam fails the test when Eve suggests he should eat it too.

So, this human instinct toward disobeying God, and being attracted to evil, is a Christian way of explaining why so many people suffer - it is because of the evil choices they make or are made by others on their behalf. God punishes them by banishing them from Eden, making them mortal, giving them work to survive and, because Eve was guiltier than Adam, women also suffer period pains and pregnancy.

Well, I thought you ought to know.

Now, to return to Marley's sermon, his message is the same. First, Scrooge is making evil choices which will condemn his soul to a kind of hell, like the one which Marley is trapped in. Secondly, his evil actions will dramatically spread misfortune and suffering to others. But, argues Marley, this can all be changed if Scrooge uses his own "free will" to change himself and society for the better.

Obviously, Dickens uses this Christian language to prompt his readers to do the same, with their free will.

Does Dickens Have Marxist Beliefs?

"'Business!' cried the Ghost, wringing its hands again. 'Mankind was my business. The common welfare was my business; charity, mercy, forbearance, and benevolence, were, all, my business. The dealings of my trade were but a drop of water in the comprehensive ocean of my business!'"

Dickens also uses Marley's anger to warn about the dangers of seeking profit for its own sake. But it is important to realise he is not anti-capitalist. He doesn't want employees to share equally in the profits – he just wants a fair wage.

Karl Marx and Friedrich Engels were both appalled at the same British poverty which so horrified Dickens. Only five years later, in 1848, Marx wrote **The Communist Manifesto**, an attack on capitalism. And this is the year revolutions spread across Europe.

Dickens instead opted for persuading his readers to be far more generous with their money, through "charity", but also to become much kinder people, showing "mercy, forbearance and benevolence". He uses Marley to describe this as an "ocean" of responsibility compared to the responsibility of gaining money, which is like only a "drop of water". He isn't arguing that business owners need to spend all their profits on the workers.

Marely Symbolises Regret

"How it is that I appear before you in a shape that you can see, I may not tell. I have sat invisible beside you many and many a day." It was not an agreeable idea. Scrooge shivered, and wiped the perspiration from his brow. "That is no light part of my penance," pursued the Ghost. "I am here to-night to warn you that you have yet a chance and hope of escaping my fate. A chance and hope of my procuring, Ebenezer."

Marley also symbolises regret. His punishment is not a particularly Anglican version of hell. Instead, Dickens opts for a Catholic idea, purgatory, a kind of halfway house bringing the torments of hell, but only for however many thousands of years it takes for your soul to do "penance". In other words, you take on suffering to pay for your sins and, eventually, you pay that debt and are allowed to enter heaven. This is just like paying money on a loan, a rather fitting punishment for a money lender!

Part of Marley's punishment, his "penance", is to watch his only friend Scrooge make the same mistakes he made, and be unable to warn him. Dickens introduces the comforting idea that even our dead friends and relatives will try to help us become better people, which offers us "A chance of hope".

These are not Anglican ideas, and so strictly speaking would not fit the Christian faith of his readers. Instead, Dickens uses "Old Marley", and Scrooge's old age, to ask his readers to imagine themselves as old. When they look back on their lives, what will they regret? He implies, through Marley, that we will all regret our actions, and how our lives have affected others.

A Prayer to Marley

The last reference to Marley is at the end in Stave Five, when Scrooge thanks him, **"'Oh, Jacob Marley! Heaven, and the Christmas Time be praised for this! I say it on my knees, old Jacob, on my knees!'"** This makes Marley much more important than either Christianity or Christmas in Scrooge's mind. At the end, Dickens wants us to focus on our own old age and regrets. He asks us to imagine how horrified we might be if we look back on lives which have made no positive difference to others.

At the end, Scrooge has learned Marley's lesson, **'"It is required of every man," the Ghost returned, "that the spirit within him should walk abroad among his fellowmen, and travel far and wide; and if that spirit goes not forth in life, it is condemned to do so after death. It is doomed to wander through the world—oh, woe is me! —and witness what it cannot share, but might have shared on earth, and turned to happiness!"'**

If we focus on just the ending here, it will fit every essay. Mankind's moral duty is to make sure that each life a person affects should be **"turned to happiness"** as a result of our attitude and behaviour. It is our duty to make others happier.

The Ghost of Christmas Past

It is difficult to decide what Dickens wants us to make of this bizarre ghost.

its belt sparkled and glittered, now in one part and now in another, and what was light one instant, at another time was dark, so the figure itself fluctuated in its distinctness: being now a thing with one arm, now with one leg, now with twenty legs, now a pair of legs without a head, now a head without a body; of which dissolving parts, no outline would be visible in the dense gloom wherein they melted away. And in the very wonder of this, it would be itself again, distinct and clear as ever.

In the flickering of "light" and "dark" it mimics a candle flame. But it also suggests the Christian symbolism of light and darkness, the battle of good and evil for Scrooge's soul.

Memento mori

It is also horrific, being described as a series of dismembered parts, even "a head without a body". Perhaps this is a warning of death to Scrooge. The Victorians had a name for this from the Latin: Memento mori. This meant a symbolic or artistic reminder of death.

Christians in particular used the idea as a reminder that they might be judged by God at any time. This makes the need to live a good, Christian life, more urgent. We might argue that the speed of the ghost's shapeshifting, which Dickens emphasises with the repetition of "now", conveys the speed at which the "light" of his life can be snuffed out by the "dark" of death.

Throughout all the descriptions of him, we can recognise aspects of a candle. Notice how the limbs suddenly "melted away". The allusion to a candle is also a Christian symbol - this is literally why candles are lit in church, to symbolise God's light and salvation.

A wider literary allusion is to the candle symbolising the brevity of life. A candle lasts a very little time, burns brightly, and then returns to darkness. This reminds a Victorian reader of another Latin phrase, carpe diem, or seize the day. It means make the most of today's short time, because tomorrow may never arrive. Both ideas are relevant to Scrooge and his need to change his ways.

Scrooge's humour as a defence against the ghost

[Scrooge] then made bold to inquire what business brought him there. "Your welfare!" said the ghost. Scrooge expressed himself much obliged, but could not help thinking that a night of unbroken rest would have been more conducive to that end. The Spirit must have heard him thinking, for it said immediately: "Your reclamation, then. Take heed!"

Scrooge's attitude to the ghost is full of mischievous humour. The idea that he would be better off (his "welfare") with a good night's sleep "of unbroken rest" rather than being dragged out of bed by three successive ghosts, is something we might all think in his position. It also reveals his complete lack of fear of the ghost.

Remember, he also used this humour when he told Marley's ghost, **"there's more of gravy about you than the grave"**. While it is tempting to see this as false bravado, simply trying to make himself seem brave and calm, there is also the possibility that this bravery and calmness are real.

This is quite a subtle trick. He makes us identify with Scrooge's sense of humour, because he wants his readers to find something in common with Scrooge. By the end of the chapter Scrooge will have lost all his composure, and will actually physically attack the ghost.

Dickens Challenges his Readers

Seeing this transformation in Scrooge is perhaps aimed at making his readers wonder if they too should also change. A typical Victorian reader would probably be certain that the poor were 'undeserving' of charity. Politics at the time suggested they simply didn't work hard enough. Whereas a middle-class reader would look at their own good fortune and decide it was all a product of their hard work and excellent financial planning.

The Spirit dropped beneath it, so that the extinguisher covered its whole form; but though Scrooge pressed it down with all its force, he could not hide the light, which streamed from under it, in an unbroken flood upon the ground.

The ghost looks so much like a candle that Scrooge believes he can be extinguished. Why does he want to put it out? It is because he can't bear to confront his past. Scrooge's distress is psychologically very convincing: he can't bear to see Belle happy with her new family, because he knows that family could have been his (as we saw in the section on Scrooge).

The role of the Ghost of Christmas Past is obviously to help us understand Scrooge and sympathise with him. But it is also to help us understand ourselves. When Scrooge re-examines his past, and begins to transform, Dickens encourages his readers to think more about their own pasts.

Scrooge doesn't want to face his past, because he doesn't want to change. He has developed his harsh persona as a response to the pain of abandonment in his youth. He wants to protect himself from further emotional pain.

The Ghost Foreshadows Scrooge's Transformation

However, Dickens uses the description of the ghost symbolically to show that Scrooge will be powerless to resist change: **"he could not hide the light"**. Then the power of this light is conveyed with **"streamed...in an unbroken flood"**. This implies that Scrooge will be overwhelmed. But, because the light is associated with goodness and Christian salvation, Dickens uses the image to suggest that Scrooge will become good, and be saved by the end of the novel.

It was a strange figure-like a child: yet not so like a child as like an old man, viewed through some supernatural medium, which gave him the appearance of having receded from the view, and being diminished to a child's proportions.

Dickens chooses to make the ghost both "like a child" and "like an old man", perhaps to remind us that we are all created by our childhoods. The ghost's size is "a child's proportions". This reminds us that childhood itself is important, not just Scrooge's childhood.

We can imagine that Dickens was totally aware of the impact of childhood, especially childhood trauma. He wrote about his own childhood poverty in **Great Expectations** and **David Copperfield** as major parts of the plot. But he kept the details of his father's debt and imprisonment a secret. He wasn't trying to reveal his own life, but the idea of cause and effect, how our psychology is created by our childhood experiences.

Christkindl

The childlike appearance of the ghost is also deliberately Christian. All things German were becoming fashionable, because Queen Victoria had married the German Prince Albert three years earlier, in 1840. He also popularised the Christmas tree, which was a relatively new addition.

Dickens uses the German (and European) tradition of the gift giver. There was no Father Christmas in Dickens' time! Instead, the German tradition was that presents were delivered by the invisible Christ-child, or Christkindl, whose presence was announced by a bell: (notice how the ghosts are all summoned by the bell of the clock).

Dickens plays with this religious symbolism to remind his readers of their Christian duty to give - in this case, give charity to the poor. They should also, like Scrooge in Stave Five, treat the poor as they would their own family.

How Scrooge Becomes Like the Ghost or Christkindl

We can also see the impact of this ghost in Stave Five. Its shape shifting between child and old man is deliberately repeated in Dickens' description of Scrooge who comments on this strange state of his as both old man and baby, **"I'm quite a baby. Never mind. I don't care. I'd rather be a baby."** In this way, Dickens keeps reminding us how important it is to re-examine our past. He may also want us to become more childlike in our outlook, pursuing joy and pleasure in simple things like family - just as Bob and Fred do. Or to take joy in play, as Bob does with his slide, and both he and Fred do with Blind Man's Buff.

Obviously, it goes without saying (but I am saying it anyway), the light symbolises Christian faith and hope. This is juxtaposed throughout the novel with the darkness and fog of London, again implying how Scrooge's transformed persona will also bring light and goodness to the world.

The Ghost's Christian Symbolism

Dickens peppers his readers with Christian references with this ghost.

"He rose: but finding that the Spirit made towards the window, clasped his robe in supplication.

"I am a mortal," Scrooge remonstrated, "and liable to fall."

"Bear but a touch of my hand *there*," said the Spirit, laying it upon his heart, "and you shall be upheld in more than this!"

First, Scrooge **"clasped his robe in supplication"**, as though kneeling down before Jesus. On the one hand this reminds us of the idea of Christian salvation. On the other hand, the image is unsettling. Jesus is referred to wearing a "robe" only as a form of mockery, when he was taken to Pontius Pilate, who was the Roman governor of Jerusalem. Pilate sentenced Jesus to death by crucifixion:

"And Herod with his men of war set him at nought, and mocked him, and arrayed him in a gorgeous robe, and sent him again to Pilate." **King James Bible**

So, the robe is also a symbol of Jesus's sacrifice, death and rebirth. This cycle is echoed at the end of the Stave, when Scrooge cannot extinguish the light – the light is killed, but reborn. It is also echoed in the shape shifting of the ghost, from boyhood to old age and at the end of Stave Five, when Scrooge shifts from old man to "baby".

Next, Dickens gives Scrooge symbolic language. Instead of saying, 'I'll fall and die', he says he is "liable to fall" because he is "mortal". This deliberately echoes The Fall of Adam and Eve, eating the forbidden fruit from The Tree of Knowledge of Good and Evil. This Original Sin is what we have inherited from Adam and Eve. You met that story earlier, in the section on free will, remember? It crops up in most books you'll study (if they were written before 1900).

Scrooge therefore acknowledges his evil nature in these words. He has recognised his sin. He has already accepted that his behaviour towards his fellow man is wrong, even though he has defended it so entertainingly and forcefully in Stave One.

The Spirit's actions, "laying" his hand on Scrooge's "heart" is perhaps more human than Christian. He is asking Scrooge to feel the memories from his past as though they are happening for the first time. He needs Scrooge to reconnect with his childhood self in order to experience joy. But he also needs Scrooge to remember the serial abandonments which have caused his desperate attraction to money and his refusal to spend it, even on himself.

What Impact Does the Ghost Have on Scrooge?

"Haunt me no longer!"

This is the only ghost described as haunting Scrooge. Dickens does this to show it is our pasts, literally, which haunt us. All our mistakes, and our unhappy memories and experiences are all in the past.

Notice that the ghost doesn't haunt Scrooge with other people's experiences, unlike the ghosts of Christmas Present and Yet to Come. Dickens suggests that the only way to become a better person is to examine our pasts. Only then can we change ourselves.

And that transformation is incredibly painful:

"Why do you delight to torture me?"

(To see how the ghost chooses which moments to revisit with Scrooge, go back to the section on Scrooge).

Ghost of Christmas Present

He felt that he was restored to consciousness in the right nick of time, with the second messenger despatched to him through Jacob Marley's intervention

Dickens reminds us that the ghosts are only there as a result of "Marley's intervention" which suggests his influence is even more important than the spirits. In the Scrooge section, I argued that it is in Stave Three that Scrooge's conversion actually happens, and combining the effect of Marley and this second ghost also suggests that this is the Stave with most impact on Scrooge.

Christian Symbolism

"I am the Ghost of Christmas Present," said the Spirit. "Look upon me!"

Scrooge reverently did so.

It is easy to assume that Scrooge's reverence is caused by his Christian faith, and his understanding of the symbolism of the Ghost of Christmas Past. But remember, he tried to shut that ghost up and extinguish its light.

So perhaps his reverence is for Christmas itself, rather than Christian salvation. This would mean that Scrooge is motivated to change because it means he will be able to enjoy goodwill now, helping his fellow human beings now, not in order to protect his soul in the future. Because he wants to learn how to help improve life now for those who are living, he decides to change.

The Pun of the Ghost's Name

The ghost's name is also a pun, to emphasise this. The "Christmas Present" associated with Christmas has a totally different meaning from time – it is a reminder of the gifts we give each other. Dickens reminds his readers of the joy of giving, the joy of generosity, because this is the lesson he wants them to learn. A further level of pun here is also that the book, published to coincide with Christmas, would also be, for so many first-time readers, their 'Christmas present'.

The Pagan Symbolism of the Ghost

"I am the Ghost of Christmas Present," said the Spirit. "Look upon me!"

Scrooge reverently did so. It was clothed in one simple green robe, bordered with white fur. This garment hung so loosely on the figure, that its capacious breast was bare. Its feet were also bare; and on its head it wore no other covering than a holly wreath, set here and there with shining icicles. Its dark brown curls were long and free; free as its genial face, its sparkling eye, its open hand, its cheery voice, and its joyful air. Girded round its middle was an antique scabbard; but no sword was in it, and the ancient sheath was eaten up with rust.

Well, what do you notice about this ghost? First, the deliberate lack of clothing, **"its capacious breast was bare. Its feet were also bare"**. This nakedness might be associated with innocence. It could also symbolise a lack of interest in possessions, as though giving everything away is a "joyful" way to live. To a Victorian, the most striking allusions are actually to pagan tradition, beliefs that predate Christianity. In Britain, the worship of nature and pagan gods is portrayed in the tradition of the Green Man which Dickens deliberately alludes to with **"one simple green robe"**.

Jesus's Robe and Crown of Thorns

Some critics see the instruction the ghost is just about to give, **"Touch my robe!"**, as Christian symbolism, like Christ's robe. But the references to Jesus' robe are quite different. His own robe is described as "seamless" – in other words, so simple and cheap, that it would have just fitted over his head. This robe is tied, with a belt. As you know, Jesus had a luxurious purple robe thrust on him before he was killed. This mocked his status as 'King of the Jews', because purple was worn by kings. But Dickens deliberately rejects purple and finery in favour of green.

The "holly wreath" around his head could be a variation on the crown of thorns placed on Jesus's head as he was crucified. Indeed, the prickly leaves do suggest this. The red berries have been taken to symbolise Jesus's blood, so we can see that it fits easily into the Christian tradition.

However, Dickens' green man imagery reminds us that all our Christian symbols actually come from traditions hundreds and thousands of years older than Christianity. Holly was given as a gift in pagan times. In fact, the Romans probably established its importance, giving green branches to each other as symbolic gifts at new year.

Well, why did Dickens go out of his way to tap into pre-Christian traditions?

- To suggest that man's kindness to his fellow man has always been a virtue, and that it is human nature. It is how we should be.

- To suggest that this generosity is a British characteristic, part of our past inheritance and ancestry.

- To suggest that the church is not acting in charitable ways – that Christmas is a time when people come together to help their fellow man without the influence of the church. In other words, the church should be at the forefront of political reform, to help the poor, but has chosen not to use its power and influence this way. The church is literally absent.

Why Does the Ghost Visit the Bakers?

"Would it apply to any kind of dinner on this day?" asked Scrooge.

"To any kindly given. To a poor one most."

"Why to a poor one most?" asked Scrooge.

"Because it needs it most."

Although Scrooge and the ghost watch people going happily to church, they don't enter. Instead, the ghost takes Scrooge to a street of bakers. He does this because the poor cannot afford ovens, or properties that might have an oven. Consequently, their Christmas dinner, probably a goose, is taken to the baker earlier in the day, and collected once cooked in time for dinner. This is a gentle reminder to the reader – we know that Dickens has deliberately priced his book so that the poor will not be buying it. His readers therefore do not have to wait at the bakers for their roast. He wants them to realise how lucky they are, and to think about those less fortunate, **"because they need it most"**. The "it" is abstract, an invisible flavour bestowed by the ghost. It could represent good will, generosity, charity – all things which Scrooge will learn to give by the novel's end.

Why Dickens Wants us to Visit the Cratchits

From the bakers, the ghost takes Scrooge to Bob Cratchit's "four room" house, where both parents, Belinda, Martha, Peter, Tiny Tim, and a little girl and little boy appear to live (though Martha may just be visiting). This will provide a tremendous contrast to the lives of his readers. They arrive just after the "goose" has arrived from the bakers. The ghost's point is that the 'undeserving poor' are not a faceless group society can write off and ignore. They are actually very deserving – they are your employees, people you actually know, whose lives could be transformed by a living wage, never mind charity.

Our ghostly narrator asks us to **"think of that"** living wage by calling attention to the Ghost of Christmas Present choosing to take Scrooge to see Bob.

"Bob had but fifteen [Bob] a-week himself; he pocketed on Saturdays but fifteen copies of his Christian name; and yet the Ghost of Christmas Present blessed his four-roomed house!"

- One interpretation is that the spirit needs to bless Bob's house because he is so poor.
- Another is that even the poor still find ways to treasure Christmas and what they can give each other, even if it is, like the meal, very small.
- Another interpretation is that Bob is a symbol for all the employees his readers will have. He is asking them to think much more curiously about them, and wonder how much more than "fifteen" "bob" they would need to survive. (A bob was 12 pence by the way).

Understanding this level of poverty for the first time, Scrooge asks **"if Tiny Tim will live"**. The ghost replies:

"If these shadows remain unaltered by the Future, none other of my race," returned the Ghost, "will find him here. What then? If he be like to die, he had better do it, and decrease the surplus population."

He uses Scrooge's own words against him ironically. However, Scrooge's words outline a political view of the time, that the poor deserve their poverty, and that the number of poor people is a financial drain on the economy. The economy would be better if this surplus died. But this view was an incorrect application of the economic theory of Reverend Thomas Malthus, who wasn't proposing killing off the poor at all, as you already know.

Malthus was already dead at this time, and wasn't able to defend himself. The solutions he proposed were family planning, late marriage and celibacy, as well as education. That said, Dickens is definitely using Scrooge to address his readers here, when the ghost calls him "man". This is because many would have agreed with Scrooge that the way to avoid a Malthusian catastrophe was to reduce the poor through a natural cull.

"Man," said the Ghost, "if man you be in heart, forbear that wicked cant until you have discovered What the surplus is".

This implies that Scrooge also represents a widespread view of men, or mankind, in English political society at the time. Through the ghost Dickens describes this as "wicked".

The Four Elements

Next the ghost takes Scrooge on a symbolic journey from the wonderful fires of London: **"brightness of the roaring fires in kitchens, parlours, and all sorts of rooms, was wonderful,"** to miners working the **"bowels of the earth"**, to sailors and lighthouse men surrounded by sea and **"deafened by the thundering of water"** as Scrooge is. Then they return to Fred's house. One reason is to show the Christmas spirit reaches everywhere, no matter how remote, or how difficult the working lives of people there.

But it is also a journey through the four elements – fire, earth, water, with Scrooge's flight being air. This emphasises that Christmas, and generosity to our fellow man, is also elemental, a force of nature. It can't be denied. This also returns us to the pagan beliefs which said that there needs to be a balance in these elements, or disaster will occur. Dickens implies it is the same with people – if one element is allowed to dominate, like Scrooge's fixation on money, disaster will follow.

The Role of Women in a Patriarchal Society

The ghost also plays with Scrooge's memories of women. He takes Scrooge to Fred's just as his wife is playing a tune on the harp which Fan used to play, reminding him of his lost sister. Then he uses Fred to remind Scrooge of his lost marriage to Belle. He witnesses the courtship of Topper, Fred's friend, to one of Fred's sisters in law:

"My opinion is, that it was a done thing between him and Scrooge's nephew; and that the Ghost of Christmas Present knew it."

Dickens needs Scrooge to think about the role of women in his life. One reason is to get him to revisit his past, and notice the pattern of attachment to being abandoned. But another is to focus on the feminine – in a patriarchal society, women were not seen as equal partners as we would understand it. To Victorians, they did complete a partnership – they were thought to have qualities which improve a man.

Women were traditionally viewed as more caring, and responsive to others' needs, so that is a powerful reason to get Scrooge to focus on them.

However, it is also a patriarchal society, in which women's futures are often decided by men. Here, Fred has to facilitate the romance between his sister in law and Topper. Some sort of romantic arrangement is completed as Topper has her put on a ring and a necklace:

and further to assure himself of her identity by pressing a certain ring upon her finger, and a certain chain about her neck; was vile, monstrous! No doubt she told him her opinion of it, when, another blind-man being in office, they were so very confidential together, behind the curtains.

It is tempting to ask whether Dickens wants his readers to question how women appear to be the property of the men in their families. Dickens, as a publisher, published many female writers when many publishers wouldn't. But I don't think the novel is critical of men's superior social status.

It is probably more likely that he is, instead, drawing Scrooge to his duties in a patriarchal society – to make sure that he looks after the interests of the family. This is an instruction to him to look after Fred, his only surviving relative, as Fred looks after the women in his family.

Perhaps it is also to show Scrooge what he has lost by excluding women and love from his life. It is another way in which Dickens tells his readers to treasure time with their own families. We can also see it as a way in which he establishes Christmas traditions – blind man's buff and forfeits, as well as drinking and toasting.

The Symbolism of Ignorance and Want

The Ghost takes Dickens on a tour, lasting the twelve days of Christmas, across Britain and then the world. Dickens gives us little detail, because it has all been preparation for the unnatural and symbolic child ghosts, Ignorance and Want.

It's further proof that Scrooge has already transformed. Because it is only now, after 12 days with the ghost, that he has learned to notice poverty and injustice. This is the first time he notices **"something strange"** which has been in the ghost's robes all along. They were always there, but until he transformed, he couldn't see them:

From the foldings of its robe, it brought two children; wretched, abject, frightful, hideous, miserable. They knelt down at its feet, and clung upon the outside of its garment...

They were a boy and girl. Yellow, meagre, ragged, scowling, wolfish...

Where angels might have sat enthroned, devils lurked, and glared out menacing...

"They are Man's," said the Spirit, looking down upon them. "And they cling to me, appealing from their fathers. This boy is Ignorance. This girl is Want. Beware them both, and all of their degree, but most of all beware this boy, for on his brow I see that written which is Doom, unless the writing be erased. Deny it!" ...

The children are described in two long lists of negative adjectives, **"wretched, abject, frightful, hideous, miserable... Yellow, meagre, ragged, scowling, wolfish"** to really labour the effects of poverty on the young. Here the ghost is not really addressing Scrooge, but "man" collectively – all of Dickens' readers.

Then he tells the readers to "beware them both". He doesn't only mean that we have a moral duty not to create such poverty. He's also voicing a political warning that we will create a dangerous underclass who might turn violent and "wolfish".

When he warns **"but most of all beware the boy"**, who represents "ignorance", he is also offering a solution. Dickens believed strongly in the power of education and literacy. Educated, literate people have so many greater chances to succeed in life. If they don't have these opportunities, they will turn to violent protest or to crime.

Dickens was fascinated by the French Revolution, and would write ***A Tale of Two Cities*** in 1859. He feared revolution in Britain, and saw education of the poor as a perfect way to avoid it. Karl Marx, the inventor of communism, was writing at the same time as Dickens. He believed that the terrible inequalities between business owners and their employees could only result in violent revolution.

Perhaps Dickens might have agreed with him, which is why his main message is to reduce the inequalities. He doesn't just ask his readers to be more generous with their time, friendship and gifts to charity. His main focus is actually on Scrooge's relationship with his employee, Bob. At its heart, the story is a plea for much greater generosity to employees and to a living wage – more than "fifteen" bob a week.

The Significance of the Ghost's Final Words

Scrooge looks at the children, and asks if there is a social solution:

"Have they no refuge or resource?" cried Scrooge.

"Are there no prisons?" said the Spirit, turning on him for the last time with his own words. "Are there no workhouses?"

The ghost points out that society is harsh and cruel by repeating Scrooge's earlier question to the charity collectors. The point is to rebuke Scrooge and help him realise his error. But more importantly, it is aimed at the readers' political views and attitude to the poor. If they continue to support the workhouse as a solution to poverty, he implies, violence will follow.

Dickens might also have wanted to show his readers that this was the most important lesson from the ghost. This is why these are his last words, before he vanishes.

Ghost of Christmas Yet to Come

Semantic Field of Death

The Phantom *slowly, gravely, silently,* approached. Scrooge bent down upon his knee; for this Spirit seemed to scatter gloom and mystery.

What is Dickens playing at in his opening line?

The problem with adverbs is that they slow down time. Students often use them when they are trying to make the action sound exciting – their choice of adverbs actually has the opposite effect.

Here Dickens wants to slow down the approach of the ghost to increase Scrooge's sense of dread. It helps us focus on the pun of "gravely" which is soon going to suggest death.

It was shrouded in a deep black garment, which concealed its head, its face, its form, and left nothing of it visible save one outstretched hand. But for this it would have been difficult to separate it from the darkness by which it was surrounded.

The semantic field of death continues with "black" and "shrouded" (a shroud being a covering placed over a corpse). So, the ghost acts as a Memento mori, (a reminder of death).

Why Doesn't the Phantom Speak?

The most interesting characteristic of this spirit isn't that he is barely **"separate…from the darkness"**. Or that his face is hidden. It is that he refuses to talk.

Dickens wants us to reflect on the future. It is unknowable. It therefore has no face and no voice. All it can do is act as a warning.

In this way, Dickens asks us to prepare for a future which is always at risk of being bleak. I'm not sure how we are supposed to react to this in a book about Christmas and goodwill. It would be a strange message if Scrooge is simply terrified into behaving better, wouldn't it?

Yet let's take a step back and imagine Dickens' readers. That is exactly the message of their Christian society! Behave well, or go to hell and suffer eternal and unbearable torment.

We are used to a society where people try to do the right thing because we believe in creating a better world – #MeToo, #BlackLivesMatter, LGBTQ, stop plastic entering the ocean, recycle, listen to Greta Thunberg, stop climate change etc.

But the Victorians didn't see moral duty in the same way at all.

In Dickens day it was relatively easy for a Christian to believe that, so long as they didn't deliberately harm someone, and as long as they continued to believe in God, they would go to heaven.

And because every other person had the responsibility to do the same, it was quite easy for a person to feel morally good by just looking after themselves and their families. Never mind the poor, other people's children, the wider world.

So, one way of interpreting this very bleak ghost is to see it as a way for Dickens to tell his Christian readers to stop thinking about death as a gateway to heaven, and start thinking about death as the end of opportunity to make a difference to the world now.

This was a pretty new idea. And it is a supernatural world Dickens has created. So it would be easy for Dickens to describe an underworld, or fiery pit, or whatever version of hell he wanted. He could easily have tapped in to all that Christian belief in divine punishment.

But he doesn't. The real punishment which the ghost reveals to Scrooge is the legacy he will leave behind. How he will die, hated by most people, having made no one's life better, not even his own.

Is Scrooge a Christian?

It is also worth asking whether Scrooge is a Christian. He hasn't expressed any religious beliefs. In Stave Five, Scrooge will go to church on Christmas morning, but that could be much more to do with tradition than faith. Although there are seven references to "Heaven" in the book, Scrooge only uses the word as an exclamation of surprise when he is taken to his boyhood, "Good Heaven!" There are also no uses of the word 'hell' in the entire book.

Perhaps Dickens uses the bleakness of this ghost to attack the way the church teaches moral behaviour. When the church focuses only on the souls of individuals, and the afterlife, rather than focusing on improving society and the lives of those in "ignorance" and "want", the church helps create and maintain an unequal society. The church becomes part of the problem which creates poverty.

One way of proving this is to ask whether the Ghost of Christmas Yet to Come actually persuades Scrooge.

The key moment which makes Scrooge re-evaluate the future is his worry about the death of Tiny Tim. The Ghost of Christmas Present already told Scrooge that he would die within the year if the future remained unchanged. So, I don't think that Scrooge needs any further persuading. This suggests that the ghost exists as a Memento mori for the Christian reader.

Is This Ghost Responsible for Scrooge's Transformation?

Scrooge himself is convinced that he has already learned enough to change his future behaviour. He thinks, when he doesn't see himself in the future, that this is proof that he has in fact changed:

"It gave him little surprise, however; for he had been revolving in his mind a change of life, and thought and hoped he saw his new-born resolutions carried out in this."

The Ghost's Main Aim is to Transform the Reader, Not Scrooge

Under the pretence of needing to show Scrooge the after effects of his death, the ghost actually uses this Stave to show the reader what poverty actually looks like. So, we visit:

The ways were foul and narrow; the shops and houses wretched; the people half-naked, drunken, slipshod, ugly. Alleys and archways, like so many cesspools, disgorged their offences of smell, and dirt, and life, upon the straggling streets; and the whole quarter reeked with crime, with filth, and misery.

Notice that the description of the streets reflects the lives of the people. The personification of "houses [are] wretched", and the streets are "straggling", implies the people within then are "wretched" and "straggling".

Although people are "drunken", he doesn't imply this is because of moral weakness. They're drunk in response to their poverty, as they are "half-naked" and "slipshod". They are victims of "misery" and "crime". The area is also described as a "quarter", which shows his readers that the poor are naturally crowded into specific areas of the city, like a ghetto, which makes escape from poverty much more unlikely.

Here we meet four people, ""**The charwoman, the laundress and the undertaker's man [and] old Joe**", a dealer in stolen and other goods. They are a comic group, who justify to each other how they have stolen the dead Scrooge's belongings, without feeling any guilt because he was such an evil man, **"a wicked old screw"**.

Dickens is probably also enjoying the joke that the dead Marley was dead as a "doornail" while Scrooge is another piece of ironmongery, a "screw". This all suggests that the scene, rather than being full of horror, is playful.

Crime is Caused by Low Wages

The real horror of the scene isn't in the morals of the criminals. They are all very good natured to each other, behaving with "**gallantry**". Nor do they set out to be thieves. This is why Dickens lets us know their occupations, "**charwoman, the laundress and the undertaker's man**".

He is not implying that the working classes are natural criminals. He is showing that their incomes are so small, that crime is a necessary option for them to escape poverty. In other words, by paying low wages, we (Dickens' readers) are creating a society where crime is inevitable.

He also shows in this society that crime does not pay. This isn't a moral argument, but an economic one. "Old Joe" is still having to work at buying stolen goods, even though he is **"nearly seventy years of age"**. We might think that he pays the criminals so little because he is, like Scrooge, looking after his own profits. However, Dickens describes his house ironically:

"The parlour was the space behind the screen of rags. The old man raked the fire together with an old stair-rod."

He too is desperately poor compared to Dickens' readers, even after a life of crime. Dickens' implication is that we create our own social problems – it isn't human nature which causes people to turn to crime, it is poverty, and our refusal to accept responsibility for creating that poverty.

Can Scrooge Get into Heaven?

The last thing the ghost shows Scrooge is his own death, bringing him to his own grave. However, this also causes the ghost to express an emotion for the only time;

"'Spirit!" he cried, tight clutching at its robe, "hear me! I am not the man I was. Why show me this, if I am past all hope!"

For the first time the hand appeared to shake.

"Good Spirit," he pursued, as down upon the ground he fell before it: "Assure me that I yet may change these shadows you have shown me, by an altered life!"

The kind hand trembled."'

This is an interesting theological problem. Let's imagine that you have broken one of the ten commandments, or committed a crime, and been released from jail. From a strictly Christian perspective, are you "past all hope" of getting into heaven? Dickens wants his readers to answer that it is possible to live an "altered life" which will alter the fate of their soul, making up for their past sins.

A Christian reader might look at Scrooge's question to mean that he is asking for more time to live that "altered life" to store up enough good works and acts of charity to cancel out decades of indifference to the poor.

But look again. He is actually asking to change all the deaths, which is why he uses the plural "these shadows". He is not concerned with his soul, his own selfish salvation, otherwise he would describe his grave as 'this shadow,' in the singular.

Instead, he is actually asking for more time to give others a better life. This is another way in which Dickens asks his readers to help the living. It is no good looking at Tiny Tim's death and consoling yourself that his soul will now be in heaven. His life is still short, which is a tragedy and our human, moral duty, is to prolong this life, rather than celebrate his eternal salvation after early death.

Tiny Tim

How Tiny is Tiny?

So, Martha hid herself, and in came little Bob, the father, with at least three feet of comforter exclusive of the fringe, hanging down before him; and his threadbare clothes darned up and brushed, to look seasonable; and Tiny Tim upon his shoulder. Alas for Tiny Tim, he bore a little crutch, and had his limbs supported by an iron frame!

Bob is not described as a large man, so we can infer from this quite how small Tiny Tim is. He is also small in a family which is already too small from malnutrition - this is one reason Peter wears such a giant collar (apart from it being very out of fashion, because it is such an old shirt). Even the weight of the "crutch" and the "iron frame" are not heavy enough to cause Bob problems, which suggest they too must be very little and therefore light.

The Christian Message of Tiny Tim the Cripple

Somehow, he gets thoughtful, sitting by himself so much, and thinks the strangest things you ever heard. He told me, coming home, that he hoped the people saw him in the church, because he was a cripple, and it might be pleasant to them to remember upon Christmas day who made lame beggars walk, and blind men see.

This Christian message feels a bit sickly to the modern reader. We are uncomfortable seeing these sorts of words put into the mouth of a child. It doesn't feel very realistic, does it? Even worse, we might feel, what if he really believes this, that God has chosen him to be "a cripple" to teach a lesson to others?

But, consider what it was like for a Christian in Dickens' day. What would you say to your disabled child? God dislikes you? You deserve it? No, you would have to find a way to make the best of it, so that your child would see a point to their disability, rather than just see it as a failed body.

His parents have probably taught him that his disability is therefore part of God's unknowable plan. Tiny Tim has obviously looked at the biblical stories of Jesus curing the "lame" and the "blind". Instead of asking why Jesus hasn't done the same for him, he has looked at the stories as symbolic. Jesus, and therefore God, loves everyone. Dickens uses this to suggest to his readers that they too should love those less fortunate than themselves.

Tiny Tim sees God as using this disability to teach the congregation to be accepting of everyone. Dickens might be suggesting that Tiny Tim has achieved a state of wisdom, and a Stoic acceptance of what he cannot change.

Tiny Tim's Death

"If these shadows remain unaltered by the Future, none other of my race," returned the Ghost, "will find him here. What then? If he be like to die, he had better do it, and decrease the surplus population."

Tiny Tim's death, you remember, is Scrooge's turning point. He also represents fatherhood - through how Bob reacts to him, and childhood - through the comparison with Scrooge's childhood. Scrooge has learned to empathise with his childhood self, rather than hide from painful memories.

Seeing how his own father's coldness has damaged him, Scrooge realises that Bob's warmth is a perfect example of fatherhood. Scrooge is so touched by Tiny Tim's weakness that he wants to protect him, because he is reminded of himself as a boy.

Tiny Tim is an Example to Challenge Political Misinterpretation of Malthus

Political policy was that the poor were a burden on society. The Malthusian belief was, as yu know, that the poor created demand for food and resources which the country could not produce, which would make everyone worse off. Without unproductive people, everyone in society would be better off.

Politicians took Malthus's economic proof that the poor were a drain on society, and created horrifying solutions - prisons, transportation, and the workhouse. This callous attitude also led many to conclude that allowing the poor and infirm to live shorter lives, through ill health and malnutrition, was a better solution.

The ghost makes Dickens' argument that you can only have this attitude to the poor and disabled if you don't think of them as individuals, or real people. This is why he creates the Cratchit family. Many Victorians believed that the poor deserved their poverty. Here, the ghost questions this with Tiny Tim, who clearly doesn't deserve his poverty and death.

The next point of the ghost's words is to carry Dickens' message that financial help to the poor won't just give them a better life, for many it will actually mean the gift of life itself. In a world where child mortality was about 50% amongst the poor, this was a very real consequence of charity.

Why Tiny Tim's Words Convert Scrooge

"I'll drink his health for your sake and the Day's," said Mrs. Cratchit, "not for his. Long life to him! A merry Christmas and a happy New Year! He'll be very merry and happy, I have no doubt!" The children drank the toast after her. It was the first of their proceedings which had not heartiness in it. Tiny Tim drank it last of all, but he didn't care twopence for it. Scrooge was the Ogre of the family. The mention if his name cast a dark shadow on the party….

It is important that Tiny Tim's disgust at Scrooge comes after we have found out that he is both wise and uncomplaining. He appears to be very able to forgive God for allowing him to be a "cripple". In fact, he has probably never even blamed God in the first place. But he certainly blames Scrooge for his family's poverty. In this way, Dickens asks his readers to realise that poverty is even more damaging than a disability.

Dickens places Tiny Tim to appear here, because at the end of the Stave, he has planned for the ghost to reveal two more children, the figures of Ignorance and Want. He wants to force his readers to think about the poor as real people, but also as real children. Their suffering is likely to be much more moving to his readers.

"Have they no refuge or resource?" cried Scrooge.

"Are there no prisons?" said the Spirit, turning on him for the last time with his own words. "Are there no workhouses?"

When Scrooge shows his concern for Ignorance and Want it is also likely that this is because he now sees them as children. Now the ghost links Scrooge's Malthusian solution to their poverty against him. Scrooge can see that his political beliefs are wrong, because they have inhuman consequences.

Who did Dickens Use to Create Tiny Tim?

One possible source for Tiny Tim was Dickens' disabled nephew, Henry/Harry. He was the son of Dickens' older sister, Fanny, who we can easily see might be a model for Scrooge's sister Fan. This might help explain Scrooge's father-like interest in Tiny Tim. However, we can see that Dickens was passionate about the treatment of children in most of his novels. He was also passionate about poverty as it affected the young, so that he campaigned continuously to improve their education through the ragged schools' movement.

Who Does Tiny Tim Represent?

We can argue that Tiny Tim's disability symbolises the burden faced by all the poor. This symbol suggests that the poor are disadvantaged from birth. Simply asking them to work harder won't give them financial stability, as pay is so low, and their education is so limited. Dickens also emphasises this with the charwoman, laundress and undertaker's man all stealing from Scrooge's corpse. They are fully employed and work hard, but their wages are so low, that they must turn to crime. It is another way the poor are kept poor.

It's also important for us to understand that Tiny Tim is also symbolic of all poor children. Modern readers see his crutch, small size and leg iron as features which make Tiny Tim stand out. In contrast, in Victorian cities, children like him would be a common sight.

This was because malnutrition and a lack of sunlight (brought on by coal fire pollution - which also caused respiratory diseases) meant that the majority of poor children were ill. It has been estimated that 60% suffered from rickets, lacking vitamin D, while 50% might have had signs of tuberculosis.

The Importance of Food

This link to malnourishment is why Dickens makes Scrooge send **"the prize turkey"** (which is **"twice the size of Tiny Tim"**) to the Cratchits, tipping the boy who fetches it **"half a crown"**. The tip of "half a crown" is two and a half shillings. This means he gives the boy the equivalent of one day's wages for Bob Cratchit. This huge tip suggests how generous Scrooge has now become. It also helps the reader picture quite how valuable the turkey must be to deserve such a tip. It emphasises how important food is to the poor, who are literally starving. It makes the reader go back to the comedy of the Cratchit's Christmas meal and wonder how little they eat for the rest of the year.

Jonathan Swift: A Modest Proposal

The is emphasised by describing it in terms of Tiny Tim: **"twice the size of Tiny Tim"**. Perhaps this comparison is also a literary allusion to Swift's *A Modest Proposal.* In this satire, Swift suggested that the poor should be paid to breed fat babies, which they could then sell to the rich who could eat them instead of other meats. This idea of helping the poor by eating them was, of course, both disgusting and ridiculous. Many readers at the time did not realise it was a satire, and thought Swift was making a sound economic argument! Here Dickens' humorous point is that the family would still starve if they ate Tiny Tim.

The Significance of the Ending

It is significant that Dickens gives Tiny Tim the final line of the whole novel: **"God bless us, everyone!"** Obviously, this appeals directly to his Christian readers. It also reminds all readers that a change in their charitable giving won't just improve the lives of the poor, it will save the lives of real children. Dickens wants to give these children a human face because even the most cynical reader won't blame a small child for their poverty, no matter how much they criticise their parents.

Dickens emphasised that by giving Scrooge his transformation in Stave Three, when he asks the Ghost of Christmas Present if **"Tiny Tim shall live"**. Scrooge wants to stay alive, not for himself, but to help the poor, and Tiny Tim in particular. Giving him the final line highlights how important children should be.

Dickens makes sure that we understand this with the narrator's description in the change in Scrooge. **"and to Tiny Tim, who did not die, he was a second father"**. We can see that becoming a father figure to Tiny Tim has become his main motive in reforming. It also reminds us of the terrible absence in Scrooge's life, which the Ghost of Christmas Past showed us - his own father.

The final clue of how important this was to Dickens, is that this line was not in the first draft. Dickens wrote and published in a rush, and this was one of the only changes he made – it was that significant for him.

He makes sure we understand that fatherhood is a main theme of the novel.

The Narrator

The Ghost as Teacher

Dickens takes the unusual step of making his narrator a character in the novel. He is a ghost. You might not have spotted this, but he tells us he is standing invisibly beside us, **"Scrooge, starting up into a half-recumbent attitude, found himself face to face with the unearthly visitor who drew them: as close to it as I am now to you, and I am standing in the spirit at your elbow."**

Within the world of the novel, Marley shows us that ghosts are either teachers, like the spirits of Christmas, or condemned to walk the earth desperate to make amends for their mistreatment of others while alive, like him, the dead business men, and the dead government.

Alternatively, he may be a ghost who is having to atone for his sins in life, which we might easily imagine involved an exploitation of young women. This is a decision you will have to make for yourself. In the patriarchal world of the novel, such exploitation can't have been considered too much of a sin, as this ghost enjoys the opposite of Jacob's misery - he appears to enjoy every minute of being a ghost. Perhaps he is best seen as a teacher, like the spirits of Christmas. He is a gentler ghost standing at our "elbow" because we are nowhere near as selfish as Scrooge. But, the narrator suggests, we still have a lesson to learn; our selfishness is still too great, so his story is here to teach us how to be better.

The Narrator and the Patriarchal View of Women

The narrator clearly plays the role of teacher, telling us the tale of Scrooge, in order to change our behaviour towards the poor and working classes. He is also, however, very excited whenever we meet a young woman, in a way which strikes a modern reader as inappropriate. He describes Fred's sister in law:

"She was very pretty: exceedingly pretty. With a dimpled, surprised-looking, capital face; a ripe little mouth, that seemed made to be kissed—as no doubt it was; all kinds of good little dots about her chin, that melted into one another when she laughed; and the sunniest pair of eyes you ever saw in any little creature's head. Altogether she was what you would have called provoking, you know; but satisfactory, too. Oh, perfectly satisfactory."

First, she is judged on her looks, and "pretty". Then her expression is permanently "surprised-looking" as she is not too intelligent. Being "exceedingly pretty" presumably means she needs no intelligence to thrive in this patriarchal society. Her mouth is not just attractive, but it appears bred for the enjoyment of men, "made to be kissed". The idea of her being bred is also continued by describing her as a "little creature", bred to arouse sexual desire, which is why she is described as "provoking" even though, it appears, she hasn't said a single word. He imagines God has made her simply for men's pleasure.

Then the narrator repeats that she is "perfectly satisfactory" as though she is a gift he has just purchased. This repetition, and the exaggerated "oh" is clearly to provide some distance between Dickens and his narrator. Even a patriarchal audience would see this as an example of too much sexism, too much viewing a woman as having a primary role to satisfy men. Remember, our narrator is a ghost, and therefore long dead. Dickens is certainly giving him a perspective from the past - his readers would recognise it as the sexist views of a bygone era. But how sexist is difficult to say.

Literary Allusions

Dickens is also playing a literary game of allusions here. An old misanthropic character who is shown visions - by goblins instead of spirits - also featured in Dickens' **The Pickwick Papers** in 1837. His family Christmas scenes are based on stories from the same book.

However, the lust filled blind man's buff scene was borrowed from a book, published in 1822, and widely read: Washington Irving's **The Sketch Book of Geoffrey Crayon**. The seduction scene with Topper and blind man's buff is almost a direct copy. This is a fascinating decision which might disappoint as many readers as it delights.

My personal feeling is that this is part of his revenge on America, which he toured in 1842, a year before. American publishers were cheating him out of a fortune, publishing his stories without paying him any royalties. Washington Irving was American! How sweet to steal some of his stories.

I think another powerful message of these allusions which, let's be honest, are pretty much copying, is to point to how Christmas traditions are also wonderful because they set out to entertain by revisiting the same experiences again and again. They are holidays which force the reader, like Scrooge, to revisit their pasts.

Dickens' Relationships with Women

Given Dickens' later history of separating from his wife, the mother of his ten children, to begin an affair with a 19-year-old actress Ellen Ternan, we can probably assume that Dickens expects us to share the narrator's appreciation of young women. When Dickens was 45, he was acting in a play with Ellen. She was 18, and had replaced another actress in the part, Dickens' 17-year-old daughter.

Their affair began in 1857, 13 years after **A Christmas Carol**. But these details suggest that Dickens expected his readers to find the narrator's fascination with young women, and his over-enthusiastic expressions of lust, simply amusing.

Society's View of Women

This helps us understand who Dickens' ideal reader was. In the 1840s, 70% of men could read, as opposed to 55% of women. It might be unsurprising if Dickens imagined a mainly male readership. However, the high price of the novel, at 5 shillings, suggests that families who bought them would all have literate women in the household, because they would all be educated.

Personally, I feel that Dickens wants us to enjoy the narrator's lusty perspective. He isn't just obsessed with young women, but also with food and, most notably, with adjectives and lists. Everything seems to him to be a symbol of fertility and plenty and more food! The narrator is a kind of proxy for Christmas - everything that Dickens wants us to enjoy about Christmas, from feasting, to party games, to courtship and romance, are all the narrator's favourites.

The Narrator's Love of Lists and Food

So, Scrooge is **"a squeezing, wrenching, grasping, scraping, clutching, covetous, old sinner!"** Even his meanness and sin are exuberant and extravagant. Marley's chain is festooned with attachments, **"cash-boxes, keys, padlocks, ledgers, deeds, and heavy purses wrought in steel"**. The effect of these lists is to portray a world overflowing with wonderful detail.

And then there is his obsession with food: **"turkeys, geese, game, poultry, brawn, great joints of meat, sucking-pigs, long wreaths of sausages, mince-pies, plum-puddings, barrels of oysters, red-hot chestnuts, cherry-cheeked apples, juicy oranges, luscious pears, immense twelfth-cakes, and seething bowls of punch."**

I think we are supposed to rejoice in all this abundance and excess.

Why is Scrooge an Oyster?

One of his most memorable descriptions of Scrooge ends hilariously with he **"was as solitary as an oyster."** Many readers tie themselves in knots trying to show that an oyster is a terrific description of Scrooge, because he is solitary. He is, but oysters are not. Dickens grew up on the Kentish coast - even today you can visit oyster fishing ports, where beaches are carpeted in oyster shells. They are one of the least solitary creatures you can find.

Even in London, oysters were always sold in cup sized portions - they were cheap food for the poor, on sale from oyster stands on the roadside. The effect of this simile is to make us laugh - the narrator picks on the oyster because he can't help himself thinking about food.

(Before I went to Kent to research this, I also tied myself in knots explaining that each oyster had the potential for a pearl - a symbol of Scrooge's potential transformation. But Dickens doesn't even mention a pearl, and the idea would certainly have been ludicrous to the working classes, who didn't treat oysters as the Victorian equivalent of buying a lottery ticket).

The Narrator's Appetites

We have many more examples of his foodie obsession. Look at his excitement in describing **"ruddy, brown-faced, broad-girthed Spanish Onions, shining in the fatness of their growth like Spanish Friars"**. The personification conveys their fatness and perhaps help us picture the narrator. The onions then behave with the narrator's familiar lust, **"winking from their shelves in wanton slyness at the girls as they went by, and glanced demurely at the hung-up mistletoe"**. Perhaps the comparison to a friar also suggests that the narrator's lust is not threatening - it is a desire he won't act on, just like a lusty friar or monk.

Later, he describes the turkey as **"twice the size of Tiny Tim"**, to show how little it would take to make Tiny Tim healthy - far smaller gifts of generosity would do it, which nudges the reader toward charity and fair wages.

He over exaggerates its size in other ways, **"He could never have stood upon his legs, that bird...He would have snapped 'em short off in a minute, like sticks of sealing-wax."** This again is deliberately humorous - the turkey obviously did walk on its own legs: there were no battery farms in Dickens' day.

But why does he pick on "sealing wax" as his simile? Perhaps it is a knowing wink to his readers that the book is nearly over, and he is about to seal the manuscript before delivery to his printers.

The Narrator also conveys the excitement of food when he takes Tiny Tim to hear the steam heating the Christmas pudding: it is described exuberantly as **"singing in the copper"**. He focuses on the sound as joyful, to emphasise the joy of the food. He also wants his listeners to appreciate the poverty of the Cratchits, who have such luxuries so rarely, that they make expeditions within their own house to go and see it.

This obsession with food is also similar to his obsession with young girls - he keeps repeating that Fred's sister in law is "plump" in the same way that he might say she is delicious. The comparison of women to food might be partly to help us laugh at the narrator, but it is probably also a reflection of the sexism of the time.

The Narrator's Humour

Perhaps we are simply asked to enjoy this as another one of his eccentricities. Dickens wants us to focus on the narrator's eccentric humour from the beginning. No sooner has the narrator begun to tell us his story, than he immediately digresses with a consideration on which piece of ironmongery should best be used to compare to death: **"Mind! I don't mean to say that I know, of my own knowledge, what there is particularly dead about a door-nail"**.

Remember Victorian readers and performance. The narrator is clearly a character whose voice Dickens wants us to overhear, like a slightly drunk uncle at a Christmas party.

We can also imagine Dickens poking fun at his own long-winded way with a story. His readers expect novels written in 5000-word sections, published weekly. His normal way of working was to hit the word count, entertain, and not finish the novel too quickly - to get his money's worth out of it, as he got paid for each instalment. As a young man I couldn't stand reading his novels, because I felt they never got to the point.

This novel is the opposite experience - written in one month, published in one text, and only five chapters long.

The Narrator's Triumph of Tone

Scrooge is like a villain on stage in a melodrama, evil in his actions but at the same time an anti-hero who we warm to. Professor Michael Slater calls this "first and foremost a triumph of tone", which of course is created by the narrator.

The easiest way to spot this is in the ending, where Scrooge offers a running commentary on everything himself. Instead of having to tell us what Scrooge is thinking and feeling, the narrator describes him speaking to himself ridiculously:

"I don't know what day of the month it is!" said Scrooge. "I don't know how long I've been among the Spirits. I don't know anything. I'm quite a baby. Never mind. I don't care. I'd rather be a baby. Hallo! Whoop! Hallo here!"

Have you ever heard a person yell out "hallo" to themselves? Or indeed, the word "whoop"? (The only time it happens in my life is when my son yells "whoop, whoop" and the job of anyone in earshot is to yell back, "that's the sound of da police", which, coincidentally, was the theme song to **Attack the Block**, a film in which my sister acted in one of the few non-Spanish roles of her career. This, btw, is a digression, in the spirit of our narrator. See what I did there?)

The final effect is to help us hear Scrooge's transformation. Although this makes it on the one hand less believable (as no one speaks that way), it also makes it more memorable and powerful (as Scrooge seems to speak to us directly).

The narrator's final act is to suggest that we have learned his lesson. This is why he gives the final words to Tiny Tim, so that we can allow ourselves to be taught by the poor. When he says, **"God bless us, every one"** we now know what this means - we all have a duty to help the poor.

Belle

Belle and Pattern of Attachment: We also see that he is coming to a psychological understanding of his past choices. You would imagine a man over 60 (such as Scrooge) looking at Belle who must still be under 45 (considering the age of her daughter) would be transfixed at the woman he has lost. If her daughter is 16, the average age of marriage 24 then she is 40, and Scrooge may well be 65 or older - so the age gap can be very significant here. Indeed, Dickens himself was completely transformed in his desires when he fell in love with Ellen Ternan (18 when he was 45).

Scrooge realises that his choice of a fiancé at least 15 years younger than himself was always likely to lead to her choosing a younger husband and breaking off the engagement. In other words, he realises that he unconsciously chose a woman who was likely to abandon him, and repeat the pattern of his childhood. This realisation is so painful that he asks the ghost to take him away from seeing it, and feeling the pain of not being a father.

When the ghost refuses, Scrooge resorts to violence, while yelling: "Remove me!" Scrooge exclaimed, "I cannot bear it!"

Dickens uses Belle to show Scrooge the riches he could have chosen instead of financial riches. When Scrooge sees her with her family, it is only 7 years ago: **"They were in another scene and place; a room, not very large or handsome, but full of comfort,"** which implies that they are middle class, but not wealthy. They have everything they need, conveyed by "full of comfort", and also by the father's arrival. He has spent enough on gifts that the shop has had to send a "porter" to carry them.

The other form of wealth is the number of children Belle has, **"for there were more children there, than Scrooge in his agitated state of mind could count"**, which is a deliberate contrast with what we imagine Scrooge would normally count - his money.

But her greatest wealth is in having children who will become companions in old age: **"and when he thought that such another creature, quite as graceful and as full of promise, might have called him father, and been a spring-time in the haggard winter of his life, his sight grew very dim indeed."**

This is the most painful moment shown to him by The Ghost of Christmas Past, and forces Scrooge to attack the spirit. As he says, **"I cannot bear it!"** As we saw in the section on the Ghost of Christmas Past, his pain is caused by his desire to be a father.

Dickens lets us know that this memory, of choosing not to have a family, is even more painful than losing Belle's love.

Dickens also uses Belle to help explain Scrooge's pattern of attachment, as we have seen. The chronology tells us that she must be much younger than him, and therefore always more likely to choose a younger husband.

It is very easy to view Belle's assessment of Scrooge's character, becoming obsessed by "Gain" and losing his love of her, replacing it with the other "idol" of "golden" money, as the view Dickens wants us to share.

She tells Scrooge she knows he will still marry her, as that was their "contract", but will then always resent her: **"if for a moment you were false enough to your one guiding principle to do so, do I not know that your repentance and regret would surely follow? I do; and I release you."** This "regret", she feels, would be that he had married someone poor, "a dowerless girl".

Another way to read Belle's words is that she has been unfair to him. He tries to speak in reply to her accusation, but she cuts him off. **"You may—the memory of what is past half makes me hope you will—have pain in this. A very, very brief time, and you will dismiss the recollection of it, gladly, as an unprofitable dream, from which it happened well that you awoke. May you be happy in the life you have chosen!"**

But, she could be completely wrong. She imagined that he wants a "contract" with a wife who will bring a "dowry". But no, Scrooge never gets engaged again. She assumes he will "have pain" for only "a very, very brief time", though we can see that he has lived the whole of his subsequent life in pain. This is why he refuses any further emotional contact with anyone.

At this stage she accuses him of already choosing to be alone and a miser, **"in the life you have chosen"**. But that is putting the cart before the horse - he has not chosen to leave her, it is the other way around.

We also appreciate the irony of **"May you be happy"**, because Scrooge himself told us in Stave One **"I don't make merry myself at Christmas"**. We realise he refuses to allow himself to be "merry" in case that too is taken away from him.

Dickens shows us this immediately in Scrooge's desperation to escape seeing this moment, **"Why do you delight to torture me?"** And we also see it in Scrooge's life choices, never to risk such pain again, and refusing to be engaged a second time, or to marry.

So, Dickens uses Belle to offer proof to Scrooge that life is a series of tragedies, in which those he loves will continually abandon him.

The Tragedy of Her Name and Dress
A "Belle" in English means a beautiful young woman. But this is not how he uses her name here. Instead, her looks are described as simply blonde, **"a fair young girl"**.

In the section on Time, you will see that bells are used as a symbol. Here, the name suggests that time was running out for Scrooge from the moment he fell in love with her. It suggests that the relationship was always doomed (as we saw earlier) because he chose a much younger partner. Dickens also emphasises this symbolically in her clothes. Rather than dress her attractively, he places her **"in a mourning-dress"**, which also symbolises their doomed relationship.

Mourning in the Victorian Era

Following a death in the family, a woman was required to wear a mourning dress. Here it is probably for a parent, and **The Workwoman's Guide**, published in 1840, suggested that it should be worn for 6 months to a year.

Obviously, Dickens also uses this to symbolise the death of Scrooge's love. But he also uses it to suggest another motive for Belle's breaking of the "contract". The grief of losing a parent ought to make her more reliant on the economic safety of her fiancé, as well as the emotional support of the relationship. However, it has also highlighted the age gap. She might now associate the age of her dead parent with the age of her fiancé, Scrooge.

Context

Dickens Needed Money

Every night, Charles Dickens walked the streets of London, often walking between 15 and 20 miles. This is where he mapped out his stories and rehearsed his characters. In October of 1843 he was particularly worried. His tour to America in 1842 had cost him money, and he was astonished that American publishers ignored his copyright, simply stealing his work. His latest novel, **Martin Chuzzlewit**, was selling badly. And to top it off, Christmas was coming, and he was expecting a fifth child – another mouth to feed.

Money, money, money he was thinking, as he walked London's streets. His first stroke of genius was to turn his desire for money, and the constant fear of poverty, into Scrooge, a miser who gives up on love and family in order to horde money.

The Christmas Branding

His second stroke of genius was to reinvent Christmas. The Decembers of 1842 and 1843 were two of the mildest ever recorded. The snow and frost of **A Christmas Carol** is thought to refer back to the period 1837 to 1841, or even the coldest period in living memory, 1810-1819. Obviously, the extreme cold is a perfect metaphor for Scrooge's cold heart and miserliness. But, on waking up in Stave Five, a changed man, it would make thematic sense to melt the snows on Christmas morning, as a metaphor for the thawing of his cold heart, transformed to a warm one. Dickens didn't do that, because this would confuse the brand of Christmas he was creating.

He had already published several Christmas themed writings and had commercial success. Making the reading public associate his story with Christmas was a brilliant branding exercise, because Christmas would boost sales every year. This is why he branded it with snow and a giant feast of a 'turkey' which, until Dickens, was not popular as a Christmas dinner. English Christmas feasts involved geese (much tastier than turkeys, but smaller).

In order to make readers return to this book, and for new readers to buy it every Christmas, Dickens tapped in to existing traditions. Instead of just being a morality tale, he tapped into our pagan past. This is why the ghosts of Christmas Past and Christmas Present make few references to Jesus or the church. Instead they suggest that light and feasting are not just symbols of Christianity, they are symbolic of man's generosity to their fellow man.

As you know, we can see this most clearly in the bare chested, holly-wearing Ghost of Christmas Present. Dickens also tapped into the winter tradition of sharing ghost stories. Just as generosity and feasting were traditions dating back long before Christianity, so was storytelling.

Ghost Stories and Victorian Entertainment

It is difficult for a modern reader, overwhelmed with choice each evening with YouTube, Tick Tock, Amazon, Netflix, TV, Radio, Podcasts, Spotify, and social media to realise how fundamental story telling has been to the human experience.

In Dickens' day it would be common to tell and read stories around the fireplace. Dickens wrote **A Christmas Carol** with performance in mind – we are supposed to hear it out loud. And the ghost story is a tradition of winter, told around the safety of the fire as the dark falls earlier and earlier and the cold literally brings death to our communities.

The Problem of the Church

Dickens' next stroke of genius came from an insult. The American newspapers, and other American writers, had accused Dickens of being money grabbing. This hurt. Dickens often saw the same complaints made by the middle classes about the poor – lazy, money grabbing, who would rather steal or drink gin than do an honest day's work. Dickens had spent part of his childhood working in appalling conditions because of his family's poverty. It astonished him that a Christian society could ignore the condition of the poor.

So, this was not going to be a mainly Christian story, as Christianity was part of the problem. The problem with Christianity, from Dickens' viewpoint, was that it told us to wait for salvation in heaven. Life can be miserable and short, the church seemed to say, but just believe in Jesus, and the afterlife will be sorted. That wasn't good enough for Dickens. He wanted to change the world, here and now.

Salvation in heaven allowed the government to ignore or mistreat the poor. As good Christians, the rich were supposed to donate to the poor, absolving the government of responsibility. Only, the rich often chose not to help the poor, who were seen as 'idle'. Dickens knew he couldn't change the government. But he thought he might be able to change the rich and the middle classes by writing specifically for them.

Normally, Dickens published books in chapter instalments in his magazine. But magazines are affordable by those on low income. Low income readers didn't need to hear his message. Just as important as making money, perhaps even more important, was Dickens' desire to change the world, so he needed to find the right readers.

The Social Experiment

This book was an incredible social experiment aimed at the well off. His next stroke of genius was to price the book at 5 shillings, making it very expensive. In just a few months after publication, a printing firm would illegally copy and sell it on poor quality paper for only 1 penny.

Yet the hefty 5-shilling price tag left him very little profit. This is staggering when we know that Dickens was in desperate need of money, yet he still insisted on really high-quality printing, and colour illustrations. He demanded 'Brown-salmon fine-ribbed cloth, blocked in blind and gold on front; in gold on the spine … all edges gilt.' Why would he do himself out of money?

Because he wanted to teach each well-off reader a lesson. This book said, loudly and clearly, 'You are well off. This book has cost you 5 shillings, compared to the 15 shillings a week for a worker with a large family like Bob Cratchit.'

So, the big payoff for Dickens would be getting enough well-off people to learn the lesson of his book. If even the worst miser, like Scrooge, could enjoy being generous to their fellow man, then so could every reader. This is why Dickens included charitable giving in the novel's circular structure – charity is rejected in Stave One, but Scrooge embraces it in Stave Five.

The Need to Influence Employers

But Dickens knew that charity alone was just the dressing on the wound. Who was causing the wound? It was the businessmen growing rich on the poverty of their workers. So, this is also a book about bosses and business owners. Why do people need charity in the first place? Because businesses do not pay a decent wage. For this reason, Dickens begins his novel with the ghosts of businessmen doomed to travel a kind of purgatory in search of release from their crimes. It is why Scrooge is not just a miser, but a boss who has to exploit his vulnerable yet noble employee, Bob Cratchit.

This is also why Dickens created Fezziwig, the antidote to the money grabbing businessman. Dickens wanted to show that bosses who embrace life, and get the most pleasure from life, are those who share their fortune, and give others pleasure.

Education

Dickens then comes up against the other problems of society, which is illiteracy and a lack of education. Poor people had to send their children to work. Astonishingly, the government saw little wrong with this. In 1844, just after **A Christmas Carol** was published, the 1844 Factories Act decided to make children's lives much better. Children aged 9 to 13 were now protected. They could **only** be made to work 6 days a week, instead of 7.

And they **only** had to work 9 hours a day.

Dickens interrupted writing a political pamphlet, *An Appeal to the People of England, on behalf of the Poor Man's Child* to write his novel. He took this political message, and created Tiny Tim. We could argue that, without Tiny Tim, the ghosts would not have persuaded Scrooge of the need to change.

Dickens' book is part of a political movement which only just over a year later resulted in Marx and Engels writing **The Condition of the Working Class in England**, which led to the principles of socialism and communism.

Dickens dramatised his political message through the Ghost of Christmas Present. He shows Scrooge a vision of reality in two terrible, starved looking children, a boy and a girl, called Ignorance and Want.

"They are Man's," said the Spirit, looking down upon them. "And they cling to me, appealing from their fathers. This boy is Ignorance. This girl is Want. Beware them both, and all of

their degree, but most of all beware this boy, for on his brow I see that written which is Doom, unless the writing be erased.

They are, of course, totally irrelevant to Scrooge's journey. The plot would be the same without them. They only exist to show that education is the solution to mankind's problem. The warning sounds like revolution. Unlike Marks and Engels, Dickens wanted to avoid a revolution.

And guess what, only 3 years later, revolution spread across Europe like an infection. In 1848 a series of revolutions swept through Europe in France, Germany, Italy and parts of the Austro-Hungarian Empire, but not Britain. This is the 'doom' the ghost foretells, caused by 'Ignorance and Want'.

It would be wonderful if the massive increase in literacy in Britain was partly responsible for the British finding a political and social voice which meant that revolution was not needed. People like Dickens believed the world could be made better, and education and literacy allowed the worker to make their own lives better.

In 1820, the literacy rate was 53%. By 1851, this had risen to 62%. Before 1840, only 16% of working-class men who could read earned more than those who couldn't. After 1840, jobs which required literacy increased dramatically. So, by 1870, the literacy rate was 76%.

Ragged Schools

Part of his solution to "Ignorance and Want" was education. In 1846, he wrote:

> "They who are too ragged, wretched, filthy, and forlorn, to enter any other place: who could gain admission into no charity school, and who would be driven from any church door; are invited to come in here, and find some people not depraved, willing to teach them something, and show them some sympathy, and stretch a hand out, which is not the iron hand of Law, for their correction."

That word "correction" tells you everything about how the poor were judged in the 1840s. Poverty was your own fault. To get out of poverty, you had to be corrected, corrected out of your laziness, drunkenness and attraction to crime and sin.

Child Poverty

In February 1843 the ***Second Report of the Children's Employment Commission*** was published. It showed how appalling the conditions of working children were in factories across the country. Dickens intended to write a pamphlet called ***An Appeal to the People of England, on behalf of the Poor Man's Child***, but instead decided to make damaged childhood a theme of ***A Christmas Carol***, through the figure of the boyhood Scrooge, Tiny Tim and the ghosts, Ignorance and Want.

1843 - He visited the Cornish tin mines. Here Dickens was appalled at the child labour and the dangerous working conditions they were exposed to.

1843 - After this he visited the Field Lane Ragged School. The ragged schools were set up as charities to educate the children of working-class people. The idea was that literate and numerate children would be able to find better, and safe employment, and improve their own economic prospects. This is why Dickens creates the figures of Ignorance and Want as child figures.

On the 5th October 1843 at the Manchester Athenaeum, Dickens gave a speech on the importance of educating the poor - this is a reason for the appearance of Ali Baba and Robin Crusoe as a real people in Scrooge's young imagination and memory. It illustrates the transforming power of literacy to literally bring other worlds to life.

Context of Poverty

The 1840s have been called 'The Hungry Forties' by historians, because there were such food shortages and mass starvation, particularly in Ireland where up to a million died. Millions of Europeans emigrated to America.

The Chartist Movement also mobilised millions of people to sign petitions and attend meetings and marches demanding greater access to the vote (at the time you had to own housing to vote). The Chartists also wanted normal workers to have the right to become MPs. To be an MP, you had to have an independent income - there was no salary for an MP, so only the very rich could make decisions in parliament. The rich did not really understand anything about what it was like to be poor.

This is very relevant to The Ghost of Christmas Present's warnings about Ignorance and Want, and also to Dickens' determination to write for property owners - they are the ones who are employers and voters. So, they are the ones his story had to reach.

Dickens's biographer, Michael Slater, describes how his visit to Manchester and Athenaeum speech on 4th October inspired Dickens to want to "to open the hearts of the prosperous and powerful towards the poor and powerless".

Dickens' Introduction to A Christmas Carol:

"I have endeavoured in this Ghostly little book, to raise the Ghost of an Idea, which shall not put my readers out of humour with themselves, with each other, with the season, or with me. May it haunt their houses pleasantly, and no one wish to lay it.

Their faithful Friend and Servant,

C. D.

December, 1843."

He wants his ideas to haunt us, like a ghost. Just as the ghost of Marley has been haunting Scrooge, unnoticed for seven years, so **"the ghost of an idea"** will take time for the reader to perceive.

This is an invitation to look more closely. My interpretation is that this "Ghost of an Idea" is the need to pay higher wages, to transform the lives of the working poor.

Malthusian Economics

Thomas Malthus, in an *Essay on the Principle of Population* in 1798, argued that population would always expand quicker than the improvements in agriculture to grow food. Therefore, the poor would end up consuming more than could be produced, and in particular more than they could produce from their work or earnings. This meant that the children of the poor would remain poor, and each generation would be poorer than the last.

Politicians chose to interpret this as proving the need to make the lives of the poor very difficult, through the creation of workhouses. These were also single sex, which would minimise the reproduction of the poor (through sex). Poor people, dying from ill health and malnutrition, would then become a solution to the problem of too many poor citizens.

Malthus himself didn't propose such inhumane ways to get rid of poverty. He actually favoured job creation through public and private building projects. He wanted the middle classes to spend more:

"the principles of saving, pushed to excess, would destroy the motive to production" he said in his later book, "**Political Economy Considered with a View to Their Practical Application (1820)**".

In other words, he wanted those with money to spend it on construction, projects and services, so that the poor could be employed and contribute to the economy. Scrooge is actually the sort of saver, a miser, who would have horrified Malthus.

Pollution and Disease

Every home was heated by coal fires, often in every room. This meant a constant belching of smoke, which meant that for much of the year, the sun was obscured. A lack of vitamin D (which we get from sunlight) was therefore common, causing rickets, and poor physical development.

In cities it has been estimated rickets affected between 50-80% of children. Tuberculosis in some form also appears to have affected about 50% of children. Many readers see Tiny Tim as suffering from both of these conditions.

Christmas

Seeing the success of Christmas stories, especially those which didn't all involve Christian stories, Dickens wrote more: *The Chimes* (1844), *The Cricket on the Hearth* (1845), *The Battle of Life* (1846) and *The Haunted Man and the Ghost's Bargain* (1848). None are famous now because they were money-making exercises, but it gives us an insight into how these were different from his motives in *A Christmas Carol*.

It is tempting to see the high price of the book (at five shillings) as proof that Dickens was mainly motivated by profit. However, he insisted on luxurious production materials: "Brown-salmon fine-ribbed cloth, blocked in blind and gold on front; in gold on the spine ... all edges gilt" (gold leaf edges)".

Then there were the costs of John Leech's illustrations. The limited print run of 5000 copies also meant that his main motive was not profit. His larger motive was to reach those 5000 wealthy readers who could make a difference to the poor and working class.

In May 1843 he attended a fundraising dinner which was filled with such rich readers, and Dickens was disgusted by them. He described these to his friend as:

"sleek, slobbering, bow-paunched, overfed, apoplectic, snorting cattle", and we can see these men satirised in the traders Scrooge visits with the Ghost of Christmas Yet to Come.

The Cratchits' House

In 1822, ten-year-old Dickens moved with his family to 16 Bayham Street, Camden Town, in London. Dickens would later describe the area "as shabby, dingy, damp and mean a neighbourhood as one would desire to see." He used the house as a model for the home of the Cratchits in **A Christmas Carol**. Dickens would later use the house again as the home of the Micawbers in **David Copperfield**.

Alcohol

There was a strong abstinence movement to make people give up alcohol, and Dickens disagreed with it. He wrote to one supporter of abstinence:

> "I have no doubt whatever that the warm stuff in the jug at Bob Cratchit's Christmas dinner, had a very pleasant effect on the simple party. I am certain that if I had been at Mr Fezziwig's ball, I should have taken a little negus -- and possibly not a little beer -- and been none the worse for it, in heart or head. I am very sure that the working people of this country have not too many household enjoyments, and I could not, in my fancy or in actual deed, deprive them of this one when it is so innocently shared."

This is why he ends the novel with a joke about abstinence. The other clue you'll need is a pun on the word "spirits" which, so far in the novel, has always meant ghosts. But the other common meaning is strong alcohol such as whiskey, brandy and gin.

"He had no further intercourse with Spirits, but lived upon the Total Abstinence Principle, ever afterwards".

Here, Dickens means that Scrooge is refusing to have anything to do with ghosts, and implies he'll keep drinking the spirits!

Warren's Blacking Factory

Dickens was sent to work here when his father was imprisoned in Marshalsea Prison for debt. This gave him a lifelong hatred of child labour, and how this damaged their education and chance of escape. He worked ten-hour days, six days a week, earning six shillings a week. To put this in perspective, **A Christmas Carol** cost five days' wages.

Not only did 12-year-old Dickens have to support his family with this money, he also had to pay for lodgings close to work. Most of the rest of the family had to live with his father John, in the prison.

We can see this could easily inform Dickens' perspective on the role of a father. He later wrote, "It is wonderful to me how I could have been so easily cast away at such an age." At least, once his father was released from prison, his parents eventually released him from the blacking factory. But, it seems, his mother had got used to her 12-year-old child earning and was actually keen for him to continue at the blacking factory!

> "I do not write resentfully or angrily: for I know all these things have worked together to make me what I am: but I never afterwards forgot, I never shall forget, I never can forget, that my mother was warm for my being sent back."

Dickens went back to school from the ages of 13 to 15, at which point he was once again removed from school and sent to work.

Remember this when people tell you school closures have been a disaster, and your life chances have been damaged. Dickens missed year 8 and year 11, and then taught himself in the British Museum library, while still working full time in a job. Every single book he ever read at that stage is probably available on Project Gutenberg with a couple of mouse clicks. He also taught himself short-hand, so he could become a court reporter. That's the equivalent of learning to touch type at 80 words per minute, something all of us can learn to do.

After becoming a court reporter, he became a parliamentary reporter and from that became a reporter of 'sketches of everyday life' in London. From non-fiction, he moved to fiction.

The key thing to take away here is that Dickens' talent wasn't mapped out in advance. It was simply produced by very hard work, and deliberately looking for ways to improve and take control of his life.

American Tour

In 1842 he went on tour to America, a trip which did not earn him enough money. He was also horrified to see both how famous he had become and that he earned nothing from the American publication of his books and their huge sales. On his return, he wrote a travel book, **American Notes**, which did not sell well. Neither did his two novels, **Barnaby Rudge** and **Martin Chuzzlewit**.

So, on the one hand, writing **A Christmas Carol** can be seen as a desperate attempt to write something to make money. But on the other hand, we can see *all* Dickens' writing as an attempt to make money. In the list of activities above, Dickens has tried out four different experiments in earning from his writing:

1. live performance of his work in theatres,

2. serialising books as weekly chapters in magazines (often published before the ending was written),
3. collating these as a separate book once they were finished
4. and, with **A Christmas Carol**, writing a whole short novel in one draft, and publishing it whole.

I find it fascinating that Dickens didn't learn to plan a book in advance until 1846, with **Dombey and Son**. Before that, he had to wing it!

Dickens the Actor

In 1832 he wrote to the manager of the Covent Garden Theatre to arrange an audition, which he was forced to miss through illness. This is worth knowing when we think about his books being written to be performed.

He created an amateur acting troupe in the 1840s and performed all over the country, including twice for Queen Victoria and Prince Albert.

He bought an impressive, grand house at Gads Hill (now turned into a private school). His father had told him, on their walks when Dickens was a boy in Kent, that one day he might be able to afford this house if he worked hard.

But my favourite part of this story is the addition of the Swiss chalet he used to write in. It was a gift to him from a famous actor friend Charles Fechter in 1864. He lived in a huge house, but made sure he walked to work every day, through his front garden, down a tunnel he had built beneath the main road, to his chalet. When you read Dickens out loud, you can really appreciate what an actor he was.

He began performing his books on stage in 1850, and donated the proceeds to charity, but by 1858 he realised both his enjoyment and the financial rewards were huge, so started performing them as a business venture.

This is something I love about Dickens, which he has in common with Shakespeare. Every masterpiece was an attempt to give the public what they want, but in such ways that they would forever see the world in a different way. If you change the way people think and experience the world, they will keep coming back to you for more.

In 1867 he returned to America, despite suffering from ill health. He gave 76 performances over 5 months and earned an astonishing $140,000.

Themes

Social Dissatisfaction and the Poor Laws

The Workhouse

You know that Dickens was campaigning against the poor laws, and in particular the cruel conditions of the workhouse. The unemployed lead lives little better than those in prison. Men often spent their days breaking stones, so that they could be used in road building, or smashing bones to be used in fertiliser.

Women did basic cleaning and manual work, and children were often hired out to factories. Essentially, you gave up your freedom in order to have somewhere to sleep and basic food rations. Poverty was essentially being treated as a crime by society - those with wealth blamed those without wealth for being poor, and "idle people" as Scrooge calls them.

The Treadmill and the Poor Law

Malthusian economics led to Scrooge's famous words wanting to "decrease the surplus population" suggesting that the poor "had better" "die" if they refused to go to the "workhouse" or "prison". Although we see prison as a punishment for crime, the Victorians saw the real crime as laziness. This is why Dickens has Scrooge say: **"The Treadmill and the Poor Law are in full vigour, then?"** The "Treadmill" was a giant hamster wheel, on which the criminals were forced to walk because, in the collective view of society, criminals were simply lazy, and could have lifted themselves out of poverty if only they weren't workshy.

The Political Views of Dickens' Readers

So, when Dickens gives these words to Scrooge, modern readers simply laugh at his words. Not so in 1843, where a huge number of Dickens' readers would actually agree with Scrooge. They would also feel a Christian duty to give to charity, so Scrooge would also be seen as mean. But Dickens' is careful to give him enough views that many readers would agree with so that, when he is transformed into a generous employer in Stave Five, readers might think of being much more generous with the wages they pay.

Politicians at the time were so convinced of Malthusian economics they actually changed the laws to allow businesses to import food from abroad. They repealed (cancelled) the existing restrictions with the Corn Laws in 1846, even though this would lead to lower profits for British farmers.

By giving Scrooge the same views as politicians of the day (and the many readers who would vote for them) Dickens hoped to force the reader to confront their own assumptions.

Dickens Wants to Show the Poor are not Idle
- You already know that Dickens introduces the charwoman, the laundress and the undertaker's man to show that the poor are forced into crime. Can you remember?

- You should also be able to use "Old Joe" and his "parlour" and his age to comment on this.
- How will you use Peter Cratchit and the Cratchit family to also comment on the view of the idle poor?

Do the Readers Make the Poor into Criminals?

What evidence will you use to show that Dickens' readers are not paying high enough wages? (Clue, remember the price of the book, and how much Bob is paid, and why he still works for Scrooge).

The Symbolism of the Cratchits' Christmas Dinner

This is why the Ghost of Christmas Present brings Scrooge (and Dickens' wealthy readers) to the Cratchits' Christmas dinner. Like Scrooge, they will be totally unaware of what these low wages mean. That is why Scrooge is astonished to see how the Cratchits have to make do with second hand clothes, tiny meals and, of course, death due to a poor diet.

This is why Scrooge can't help asking **"tell me if Tiny Tim will live?"** It is why Dickens makes sure the answer is no - he will die unless Scrooge, and society, and in particular the readers of this expensive book, change their attitude towards wages.

Scrooge begs the ghost **'No, no… Oh no, king Spirit! Say he will be spared.'** Here Dickens (through the ghost) gives Scrooge's Malthusian words back to him: "If he be like to die, he had better do it, and decrease the surplus population."

We can see that these words are not just aimed at Scrooge, but at the political views of his readers.

Sabbatarianism (Keeping the Sabbath day holy by refusing permission for trade on Sundays)

Dickens felt the Church should encourage the government to allow Sunday trading. Believe it or not, God banned work on a Sunday as one of the Ten Commandments.

In 1836 Dickens published the pamphlet **Sunday Under Three Heads**, which opposed the idea of closing businesses on a Sunday. His arguments were about how these closures helped the upper and middle classes feel virtuous and Christian, but how the working classes were being denied all the pleasures and many of the necessities of life.

Sunday was their only day without work, and nothing was open or available to them. Whereas, the middle-class reader might not work at all, and would be able to enjoy themselves freely on Saturday, and buy what they needed in advance for Sunday. This is why Dickens includes the following accusations made by Scrooge:

"Spirit," said Scrooge, after a moment's thought, "I wonder you, of all the beings in the many worlds about us, should desire to cramp these people's opportunities of innocent enjoyment."

"I!" cried the Spirit.

"You would deprive them of their means of dining every seventh day, often the only day on which they can be said to dine at all," said Scrooge. "Wouldn't you?"

Because Scrooge is by this stage such a miserly "covetous old sinner", Dickens wants his readers to be shocked at their own cruelty. Supporting Sabbath closures would make the reader, in Dickens' eyes, a greater social evil than being Scrooge.

Theme and Context of Poverty

The Lessons of Manchester

In October, 1843, a month before writing the novel, Dickens travelled to Manchester to give a speech in support of the Athenaeum, an educational charity. He was horrified by the working conditions of children in Manchester's factories. This gives an obvious origin for the two spirits, "Ignorance and Want". This is why the original illustration, by John Leech, shows factory chimneys in the background, which look a lot more like Manchester than London.

Six months after the novel was published, the 1844 Factories Act tried to make children's lives better. Do you remember what it said about children and work?

Now children couldn't start work until they were 9! And they couldn't work more than 9 hours a day! And they had to have Sunday off! (It is bad writing to use too many exclamation marks, but...)

Victorian Death

It is worth remembering that the presence of death was much greater then. As I write, in December 2020, with the vaccine starting to be given, deaths from disease in Victorian Britain were far greater than they are now, at the height of a pandemic. In 1840, the death rate was 23 per 1000, or 2300 per 100,000.

Now, let's compare that to England in 2020, when we had an extra 100,000 deaths because of the Covid pandemic. Gov.uk gives us these statistics:

"For England, the year-to-date age-standardised mortality rate for 2020 was 1,038.1 deaths per 100,000 people, which was statistically significantly higher than all years between 2009 and 2019."

Put another way, the highest death rates in living memory, which have traumatised the country and led to three national lockdowns would, to a Victorian, have appeared a miracle of good health. They had double our rate of pandemic death every single year.

Theme of Generosity

Scrooge

Oh! But he was a tight-fisted hand at the grindstone, Scrooge! A squeezing, wrenching, grasping, scraping, clutching, covetous, old sinner! Hard and sharp as flint, from which no steel had struck out generous fire; secret, and self-contained, and solitary as an oyster.

Dickens sets Scrooge up almost as a pantomime villain. The list of five adjectives to describe his sinful greed is deliberately over-exaggerated (hyperbolic). He links these five neatly to a metaphorical "tight fisted hand", as though each of the five fingers and thumb contains one of these adjectives.

Dickens lays on the harsh consonance of 't' and 'c' and 'k' to emphasise the harshness of his personality. Then he wants us to notice the extravagant sibilance, particularly in **"secret, and self-contained, and solitary as an oyster"**. We might argue that the generosity of his language, bombarding us with these techniques, mimics Dickens's desire to make us generous with our thoughts and intentions towards the poor.

The metaphor identifying him as a fire lighting "flint" is also really clever. Dickens tells us that a flint should give "generous fire", but scrooge doesn't. This prepares us for his Stave Five transformation, because Dickens has already suggested that it is in Scrooge's nature, like a flint, to become "generous".

Fezziwig

Scrooge's transformation is also helped when he revisits the past generosity of Fezziwig. The Ghost of Christmas Past ironically plays down the generosity of Fezziwig's Christmas ball, commenting that **"He has spent but a few pounds"**. This deliberately provokes Scrooge to counter the ghost's dismissive tone:

"He has the power to render us happy or unhappy; to make our service light or burdensome; a pleasure or a toil. Say that his power lies in... things so slight and insignificant that it is impossible to add and count 'em up; what then? The happiness he gives is quite as great as if it costs a fortune."

It's easy to see Scrooge's later concerns about Tiny Tim, and his apparent breakdown when he sees his own grave, as proof that Dickens main messages are:

1. Give generously to the poor through charity - you might even save lives, especially vulnerable little children who never deserve an early death, do they?

2. Start doing this now, because your soul will probably go to hell if you don't - just look at what has happened to Jacob Marley!

The Reader

But actually, Dickens' message is also aimed more directly at the well off, or wealthy reader. As you know from the 5-shilling price tag, Dickens has used the book specifically to target wealthy readers. He knows that they, like Fred in the novel, will have employees at home: domestic servants. These readers will also have at least one employee, like Scrooge, or apprentices, like Fezziwig.

The point of this scene and this exchange with the ghost is that Dickens wants his readers to realise the enormous power they have as employers. Kindness costs very little and yet for employees, "the happiness is … great": small actions have huge consequences.

Fred

He may rail at Christmas til he dies, but he can't help thinking better of it—I defy him—if he finds me going there, in good temper, year after year, and saying, "Uncle Scrooge, how are you?" If it only puts him in the vein to leave his poor clerk fifty pounds, that's something….

Fred continues to wish his uncle a merry Christmas every year, despite the rude reaction he gets from Scrooge. Dickens doesn't just focus on this emotional generosity, on Fred's determination to be generous with his time and positivity, even when he is rejected. Fred's (and Dickens') main point is again about the role of the employer, to pay a living wage.

Bob Cratchit

In this example, Bob receives just over 15 shillings a week. There were 20 shillings in a pound, so "fifty pounds" is worth 1000 shillings! Over 52 weeks, that's 19 shillings per week. It may be that Fred is focusing on Scrooge's death, implied by "leave", so Fred wants Scrooge to give over a year's salary to Bob in his will.

Another interpretation, though, is that Dickens is suggesting to us what an appropriate wage might be, not fifteen shillings a week, but thirty-four (to make £50). Pointing out this shortfall to all his readers might make them reconsider a fair wage, to lift their domestic servants or other employees out of poverty.

The Cratchits

"I'll send it to Bob Cratchit's," whispered Scrooge, rubbing his hands, and splitting with a laugh. "He shan't know who sends it. It's twice the size of Tiny Tim…."

Dickens makes us focus on what generosity actually means. He has dragged Scrooge, and us, to the Cratchits' Christmas dinner. He has made us laugh at their poverty, without cruelty. The scene is both comic and full of pathos, as every detail from the "ribbons", to Peter's ridiculous second-hand shirt, to the handful of cups **"Two tumblers, and a custard-cup without a handle"**, to the tiny meal, and the family's refusal to commit the "heresy" of complaining, leads us to understand how the poor do not deserve their poverty.

The gift of the massive "turkey" is there to remind us that their poverty is so great that the most important gift is actually food. Simply allowing the family to eat enough also transforms

Tiny Tim's fate - he lives. It is shocking to Dickens that Scrooge can see his clerk Bob every day, and never realised that his family are close to starving.

Bob's Salary

It is also worth asking why Bob still works for this **"tight-fisted ... squeezing, wrenching, grasping, scraping, clutching, covetous, old sinner!"** The answer is shockingly simple: Scrooge is not paying low wages compared to other employers at the time. Dickens makes sure we completely understand this point when he tells us how little Peter will get when he finds a "situation" at work, of five and half shillings, about a third of Bob's wages.

Dickens wants his readers to realise that the fair wages they are paying would also seem fair to a miser, a "covetous old sinner" like Scrooge. Yes, he seems to be saying, this caricature of cruelty is no worse than you, the reader!

Jacob Marley

"The common welfare was my business; charity, mercy, forbearance, and benevolence, were, all, my business. The dealings of my trade were but a drop of water in the comprehensive ocean of my business!"

The hyperbole of this metaphor is extravagant. It isn't likely to persuade the reader to change, just as Dickens doesn't expect it to change Scrooge. But it does set out clear reasons for change, reasons which the ghosts will teach us and Scrooge. But the real skill in the scenes Dickens presents in his fictional world, is how these encounters also invite the readers to look at their own lives and the consequence of their own actions.

Society's Malthusian Justification for Criminalising the Poor

Dickens is also fighting against the political views of his society. The workhouse, prison and transportation were solutions to crime and as most crime was caused by poverty, these were seen as solutions to the poor.

Can you remember what Dickens includes in the novel to attack these solutions?

Charity

Dickens introduces two charity collectors in Stave One, and returns to one of them in Stave Five, when Scrooge gives him so much money that the collector is almost speechless, **"I don't know what to say to such munifi—"**.

Charity was seen as a moral obligation, and mentioning sums donated could be seen as boastful, and therefore immoral. Dickens has to buy into those social manners, so Scrooge "whispers" the amount, and actually prevents the "portly gentleman" from continuing and mentioning the huge sum Scrooge is donating.

Dickens actually makes fun of this reserve when Scrooge is asked in Stave One to donate,

"What shall I put you down for?"

"Nothing!" Scrooge replied.

"You wish to be anonymous?"

This misunderstanding ridicules the idea that people who give to charity should be embarrassed at others knowing. If people published how much they give, it would probably lead to a lot more giving, but Dickens knows that spelling this out would be a stop too far for his British readers!

Wages are More Important Than Charity

This allows his readers to set their own limits on what they would give to charity, and feel generous. Notice that this is the opposite of his approach to wages, where he is very precise, even to the point of detailing the pence as well as shillings. This is because charity will have little impact compared to an increase in wages - fair pay of course will lift millions of Cratchits out of poverty.

This helps explain why Scrooge desperately wants to raise Bob's wages in Stave Five, **"I'll raise your salary, and endeavour to assist your struggling family."**

Readers' Objections to Raising Wages

It is easy to dismiss this as wrapping up a kind of fairy tale ending. But look at what the narrator feels he needs to tell us next:

"Some people laughed to see the alteration in him, but he let them laugh, and little heeded them; for he was wise enough to know that nothing ever happened on this globe, for good, at which some people did not have their fill of laughter in the outset".

Dickens must have imagined the voices of his wealthy readers raising an objection to paying higher wages. If they did, their friends, neighbours and colleagues would potentially ridicule them for paying over the odds. Through Scrooge's reaction and wisdom, Dickens wants to assure his readers that making a positive difference to the lives of their employees is more important than social ridicule. He also minimises this, by telling us that only "some people laughed".

Public Ridicule

This ending does give us a real insight into the main barrier to generosity in the Britain of 1843, the worry over public ridicule and living a life in opposition to the Malthusian solutions of government.

Perhaps Dickens is also anticipating a cynical response from readers, who won't believe in his transformation, any more than they would believe in a fairy tale:

A famous critic, Edmund Wilson, called this transformation "the Scrooge problem".

"Shall we ask what Scrooge would actually be like if we were to follow him beyond the frame of the story? Unquestionably, he would relapse, when the merriment was over — if not while it was still going on — into moroseness, vindictiveness, suspicion. He would, that is to say, reveal himself as the victim of a manic-depressive cycle, and a very uncomfortable person."

This is exactly the kind of reader who will want to dismiss the idea of paying their employees a living wage, and this is exactly why he deals with the idea of public ridicule at the end of the novel.

Theme of Greed

Is this even a theme? I don't think it is, but I include it here in case it ever turns up in the exam.

Stave One
It is very easy to focus on the fact that Bob is allowed only one coal to keep warm by. But for greed to be the theme, Scrooge would need to be warming himself liberally. He isn't. He is described as "frozen" in personality, so much so that the cold doesn't appear to affect him. When he goes home, his dinner is a plate of "gruel", which is just the sort of food the poor would be served in the "workhouses" Scrooge recommends.

Scrooge doesn't live with any kind of luxury, and we might argue he gives himself few pleasures. His refusal to give money to charity does show that money is his one area of greed. This is not because he is greedy, or interested in acquiring possessions, status, luxury and leading a life we would associate with greed. We will see in Stave Two that Scrooge has a different motive for his "covetous" love of money.

The real reason he doesn't give to charity is not to illustrate his greed. Instead, Dickens uses it to show society's prejudice against the poor. This is why Scrooge refuses to contribute: **"I don't make merry myself at Christmas and I can't afford to make idle people merry"**. Society's reason is not greed, but a belief that hard work is the only way out of poverty. The Victorians made a distinction between the "idle" poor and the deserving poor. Working people with large families, like the Cratchits, were deserving. Those who were out of work were considered "idle", a drain on society.

We are all brought up to believe in the idea that our success is due to our own hard work, rather than luck. If this is true, then those who are unsuccessful must be lazy, stupid, and deserve their poverty.

This is why Dickens gives Scrooge the Malthusian idea to **"reduce the surplus population"**. This idea was also not based on greed, but a mathematical approach to economics. As you know, Malthus showed, correctly, that food production could only increase incrementally, while population increases exponentially. The only way for society to function was to limit the number of people who consume more than they produce - the poor. This is still true today, of course, the difference being how much more food we can produce.

Although Scrooge's solution is cold hearted, it is "workhouses" and "prisons". In other words, these are society's solutions. They are not motivated by greed directly, but by a desire to keep society growing at a sustainable rate.

The Victorian Household
Dickens, though, was not really interested in economics, but he was concerned about fairness.

Imagine a middle-class Victorian household. You would have a maid, who did all your cleaning. You might have a cook. You would definitely have a laundress, who would do your laundry for you, and you would employ a gardener and someone to do household maintenance when you needed it. You would probably employ a governess to educate your children, and someone to help you in the nursery with young children. Food would be delivered daily by different stores.

This meant a huge number of people you needed to pay. This is too expensive now, for the simple reason that there are fewer people to do those jobs, and we do them ourselves. But in Victorian Britain, there was no contraception. Large families were very common, and poor children would be put out to work. There was an endless supply of people to fill those roles. And, because there were often not skilled roles, anyone could do them. As an employer, there is no need to pay higher wages, if you have 50 applicants for a post. In this way, Victorian wages were kept very low.

This means that Dickens' well-off readers would not see themselves as greedy, simply as paying the going rate.

However, where Dickens is political, is when he looks at the going rate, and says to his readers (though not in these words):

Do you have any idea how poor people really are? Do you have any idea how easy it would be for you to transform people's lives by just paying a little more? No? Ok, let me create a remarkably cruel miser, who seems to hate enjoyment, and people and yes, even Christmas. I'll make you laugh at his rude, spiteful ideas, and show you a truly "covetous, old sinner". And then, then I'll show you that this wicked man actually pays his employee the going rate - he pays his staff the same as you do. What's the difference between his miserliness, and you? None! Start thinking of others. Save lives. Come on, it's Christmas.

Stave Two

Scrooge is engaged to Belle. They have had a "contract" made when they were both "poor". When she broke off their engagement, she accused him: **"Another idol has displaced me...A golden one."** Scrooge is devastated by this, even as an old man.

If Belle's accusation is correct, it would be logical for Scrooge to simply marry a wealthy woman, who would add to his own wealth. Instead, he chooses never to marry. In fact, her abandonment of him is so painful, that he tells the Ghost of Christmas Past, **"show me no more! Conduct me home. Why do you delight to torture me?"**

He is tortured because he realises he has made terrible choices in his life. But as the section on Scrooge's patterns of attachment shows, the cause of these choices isn't greed, but the relationships of his childhood repeating themselves: he keeps choosing relationships which end in him being abandoned.

Hopefully you know all this by now!

Stave Three

Some readers feel that Scrooge deliberately keeps Bob Cratchit and his family poor. But if that were the case, there would be little point in The Ghost of Christmas Present taking him to visit the Cratchits. Scrooge would just think, 'duh, that's their problem'.

Victorian Wages

Instead, Scrooge is simply paying Bob the going rate. The British Library, in an article by Liza Picard, shows that a middle-class clerk, working at a bank would earn between £90 and £100 per year. Bob, in a tiny business, which employs only him, earns £39 a year. A bank clerk would walk an average three miles to work, which is exactly what Bob walks from Camden Town. A maid-of-all-work maintaining and clearing a Victorian home would earn only £6 per year.

So, the shock for Scrooge isn't the impact of his greed. The shock, the real shock that Dickens wants his middle-class readers to realise, is that Scrooge is paying the same rate as they will be, to their staff. And as a result, the families of their employees will be poor, often ill, and likely, like Tiny Tim, to have malnourished children who die young. The shock is the injustice of the whole of society.

If we see Scrooge's problem as greed, we miss Dickens' purpose, which is to change society by changing the employers' attitude to wages.

Stave Four

The Ghost of Christmas Yet to Come shows Scrooge four people exploiting his death, by stealing from his house and corpse. It would be very easy to see these as a dramatisation of greed. They can be seen as a just punishment for Scrooge's greed, like characters in a morality play who were not really individuals, but represented different types of sin. Greed was one of those cardinal sins.

But that again would miss Dickens' dramatisation of his economic point. Listen to this:

"Let the charwoman alone to be the first!" cried she who had entered first. "Let the laundress alone to be the second; and let the undertaker's man alone to be the third. Look here, old Joe…"

- Test yourself on this; Why does Dickens name their jobs?
- The "charwoman", probably the lowest paid, has stolen the most. Dickens makes us see that crime is directly connected to poverty.
- Look at how little they actually come away with. This symbolises how little the rich actually contribute to society - they keep everything for themselves, even in death.
- How does he use Old Joe to show that crime pays very little?
- Why don't Victorian's need to increase wages to get work done?

Scrooge's Greed as a Money Lender?

Scrooge asks the ghost to take him to see someone **"who feels emotion caused by this man's death"**. Here Scrooge meets one of his own future clients, who is delighted that Scrooge has died, because it gives him more time to pay the interest on his loan (and perhaps repay the loan itself).

So here, finally, we can say that Dickens' theme is greed. But is it? The man isn't going to get a better deal, he is just going to get a "week's delay" in paying his debt. Though Scrooge might have been "merciless" in refusing, he isn't charging higher interest rates. The man certainly doesn't expect to have to pay less to another "creditor". And obviously, a money lender who charged higher interest rates than other money lenders, would soon go out of business.

So again, Scrooge's sin is not that he is greedy, but that he has not cared about the suffering his business causes other people.

Stave Five

Scrooge has a changed perspective in the final Stave, which makes him excessively generous. He donates to charity a huge sum which includes **"a great many back-payments"**. This is where the idea of greed as a theme has come from, because greed feels like the opposite of generosity.

But Dickens isn't suggesting to their readers that they should donate huge sums to charity. They won't have hoarded huge amounts of money, unlike Scrooge. They probably do give to charity already.

What they almost definitely don't do is pay everyone they employ a living wage. This is why Dickens makes us focus on Bob and his "salary". This is why the narrator feels he has to tell us that Scrooge was "wise" to ignore the ridicule he received as a result of treating Bob so well: **"some people laughed to see the alteration in him"**.

The opposite of Scrooge's generosity is not greed; it is what everyone else thinks is a fair wage. That's the real message of the novel.

Theme of Regret

Christians had been taught that their souls would live forever, either punished for their crimes in hell, or rewarded for their good actions in life, in heaven. So, Christians would regret any action which caused their soul not to enter heaven.

Dickens taps into this straight away with the creation of his first ghost, Jacob Marley.

Why did I walk through crowds of fellow-beings with my eyes turned down, and never raise them to that blessed Star which led the Wise Men to a poor abode! Were there no poor homes to which its light would have conducted me?

His first allusion to the **"blessed Star"** is the star of Bethlehem. This was the star which lead the 'Wise Men' to find the baby Jesus. Because Jacob **"never"** looked up, he suggests that he lived his life without any Christian belief.

Now, in death, he imagines that Christian faith, and God's "light" "would have conducted" him to the "homes" of the "poor". He implies that a Christian's duty is therefore to help the poor. These are the good actions which would let his soul into heaven. His regret is in two parts. Firstly, his soul has been condemned to travel in torment for 7 years because he didn't care about the poor.

Secondly, all that time he has desperately wanted to make up for this past mistake, but cannot. Dickens' point is not that you will die with regrets if you are generous in life, it is that your soul will be punished. So, being generous makes sense because, in the long run, you are really being generous to yourself.

Dickens also makes clear that Marley's fate awaits all businessmen, who make up the ghosts Scrooge is shown outside his window. This is why so many of them are "familiar", and Scrooge recognises them. Dickens wants us to know that Scrooge's sins will be similar to lots of businessmen.

Listen, he seems to be saying, let me show you what you too will regret when you are dead.

The misery with them all was, clearly, that they sought to interfere, for good, in human matters, and had lost the power forever.

Why Does Scrooge Revisit His Childhood?

Have you ever wondered why Dickens takes Scrooge back to his childhood? If all he wanted to do was show that how we behave has consequences, and that if we are more generous with our time and money, everyone will live happier lives, then why bother? The child Scrooge had no power. Indeed, he didn't make any decision to affect anyone. He didn't do anything he needs to regret.

And yet that's the first place Dickens asks the Ghost of Christmas Past to visit.

This suggests that a major theme of the novel is actually childhood and parenting. This spirit helps Scrooge realise what has caused his miserliness. He begins to understand it is about control and coping with abandonment.

Can you remember the different ways Scrooge has been abandoned?

Scrooge's father abandoned him as a child, isolating him at boarding school, while preferring Scrooge's younger sister, Fan. Scrooge has repeated this behaviour, saving his cruelty and barbed comments for males. Dickens wants us to realise that he doesn't just aim this at the powerful (and therefore men) but also at the young and powerless: boys. This is why he is so rude to the carol singer. Not because he is simply cruel, but because he is locked in to repeating the behaviours of his childhood. Because his father was cruel to him, he is cruel to other boys.

Revisiting his past, he now regrets being cruel to the boy carol singer.

"I wish," Scrooge muttered, putting his hand in his pocket, and looking about him, after drying his eyes on his cuff: "but it's too late now…. There was a boy singing a Christmas Carol at my door last night. I should like to have given him something, that's all."

Regretting the Influence of His Father; Patterns of Attachment

So, this regret is not just about his treatment of the young boy. It is also a regret about how he has allowed his father's behaviour to influence him. We will see this most clearly at the end, when Scrooge chooses the role of fatherhood for himself. He reinvents himself as a "second father" because this is the psychological lesson he has learned. He has understood what has made him miserable.

Do you remember how his visit to Belle and her family also made him regret not being a father?

[W]hen he thought that such another creature, quite as graceful and as full of promise, might have called him father, and been a spring-time in the haggard winter of his life, his sight grew very dim indeed.

At this stage in the novel, he imagines a daughter he might have had, and the father he might have been. He still can't quite imagine himself as a father of a son, which is why Dickens doesn't give Belle a son.

But at least Scrooge doesn't just feel sorry for himself, and regret that he didn't have a better father. Again, he regrets that he has been influenced by his own father. He has also realised, in Stave Two, that he has repeated his mother's behaviour of abandonment in choosing Belle, knowing it was highly likely she too would abandon him (remember that she is so much younger than him).

Regret at Not Helping Others

The most obvious image of regret is the moment Scrooge finds his own grave, and discovers that he has died unloved, unmourned and actively disliked. But we shouldn't make the mistake of seeing this as regret about his own death. Instead, he tells the ghost:

"Good Spirit," he pursued, as down upon the ground he fell before it: "Your nature intercedes for me, and pities me. Assure me that I yet may change these shadows you have shown me, by an altered life!"

He is not trying to change so that his soul will go to heaven. Instead he wants to change his effect on other people, "change these shadows you have shown me". His regret is not based on a Christian view of the world, but on a view of social justice. He wants to live "an altered life" so that he can improve the life of others.

This is why, in Stave Five, he wakes up with three aims:

1. Firstly, to save Tiny Tim from death so he sends the massive Christmas turkey "twice the size of Tiny Tim".
2. Secondly, Dickens' social message is completed when Scrooge insists on giving Bob an increase in salary.
3. But finally, on a personal journey, he becomes **"a second father"** to Tiny Tim. This suggests that his most powerful regret was how he let his own father, and his own childhood, take away the pleasures of adult life and relationships.

This also links to Dickens' powerful belief that the most long-lasting social change will happen when society treats its children better. We are reminded that the worst problem for society, an unexplained "doom" is not because of poverty and poor children, represented by "Want". Instead, it is the lack of education, represented by "Ignorance". In this way Dickens asks society to become the father to all its children and why at the time he wrote the novel he was campaigning for the Ragged schools to be funded.

That is why the Ghost of Christmas Present doesn't warn Scrooge he must change in any way. His only warning, "beware" concerns the "Doom" of ignorance. The warning means society will regret not paying attention to this, and it hints towards a warning of social unrest and revolution. Only five years later, revolutions swept across Europe, as the poor rebelled against their societies. Amazingly, Britain had no revolution. Who knows, perhaps enough people listened to Dickens' message, and made a better society.

Theme of Moral Responsibility

Changing Ideas About Hell

If that spirit goes not forth in life, it is condemned to do so after death. It is doomed to wander through the world—oh, woe is me! —and witness what it cannot share, but might have shared on earth, and turned to happiness!

Let's be clear. It isn't a part of Christian teaching that the dead become ghosts. In Catholic teaching, there is a similar idea of purgatory, a kind of waiting room between heaven and hell, where your soul is punished for its many sins, unless it was one of the big ten - murder, adultery, worshipping another god, having strong, envious desires for anything your neighbour owns, including his "ox" or his "ass". And so on. For those, you went to hell. In other words, just being mean and unpleasant - like our man Scrooge - only landed you in this kind of limbo, where your soul would do its time until God decided you had paid your debt and could enter heaven.

In Dickens' time the Anglican church (which isn't Catholic) had begun to move away from the idea of hell being a place for fire and brimstone and eternal pain and torture. This all seemed a little 'extra'. Today, the Anglican church doesn't have much to say about hell. Dickens taps in to the Catholic idea of purgatory to create a universe in which God isn't quite so binary. After all, is a rich person who has no need to steal but doesn't help the poor, morally better than a poor person who steals to feed her family when the alternative is illness and starvation?

In the binary of view of heaven and hell, yes. The poor person goes to hell. It is difficult to keep faith in a God you think is unfair, so Dickens' is playing with the idea of a fairer kind of hell, or punishment in the afterlife, based on our moral actions in real life.

The Rhythms of the Preacher

"Business!" cried the Ghost, wringing its hands again. "Mankind was my business. The common welfare was my business; charity, mercy, forbearance, and benevolence, were all my business. The dealings of my trade were but a drop of water in the comprehensive ocean of my business!"

Marley takes on the speech and rhythms of a campaigning preacher which would have been very familiar to Victorian readers. They would hear such sermons in church, and also read them in pamphlets. Here's a brief extract from a famous contemporary preacher, John Henry Newman. "**The affairs of nations, the dealings of people with people, the interchange of productions between country and country, are of this world. We are educated in boyhood for this world; we play our part on a stage more or less conspicuous, as the case may be; we die, we are no more, we are forgotten**." Notice the similar pattern of lists and repetition for emphasis, the idea that we are all connected.

Dickens uses Marley to suggest that business itself is naturally evil. Not because businessmen are evil (if they were, the ghosts wouldn't be feeling so miserable and guilty). Instead, he suggests that business makes a profit from its workers by keeping them poor. It is against "mankind" in this way.

The Problem of the Church

Dickens also deals with a tricky theological problem. The instruction to keep "the Sabbath holy" is one of the ten commandments. So, the church had a very good reason to make sure all businesses were shut on a Sunday.

However, if you had nowhere to store food, because you are poor, finding that you can't buy anything to eat because all the bakeries were forced to shut doesn't feel very Christian. So, Scrooge looks at the bakery and asks the spirit: **"You seek to close these places on the Seventh Day?" said Scrooge. "And it comes to the same thing."**

The Ghost of Christmas Present points out that many people who call themselves Christians behave in uncharitable, unkind and therefore unchristian ways:

There are some on this earth of yours... who lay claim to know us, and who do their deeds of passion, pride, ill-will, hatred, envy, bigotry, and selfishness in our name, who are as strange to us and all our kith and kin, as if they had never lived. Remember that, and charge their doings on themselves, not us.

This is a very odd conversation to have, isn't it? The ghost is trying to persuade Scrooge to be more generous. Scrooge's question attacks the ghost for not representing a kind and generous God. In reply, the ghost implies that the church is not really carrying out God's teaching. This is a direct hint to his readers that Dickens thinks that the church should have no say in making laws - Parliament could easily decide that essential businesses should be allowed to stay open on Sunday.

It is a strong hint that the church should be opposing solutions to poverty like the workhouse, transportation and prison for minor thefts. He accuses the church of "**hatred, envy, bigotry, and selfishness in our name**", meaning in the name of God.

So, Dickens was also trying to change Christian behaviour.

Pagan Values and Traditions

Of course, the other idea which is obvious to a Victorian reader, is that this ghost is more pagan than Christian. He is pointing out that the narrow interpretation of the Bible goes against humanity. It implies that pagan traditions involving generosity, like the Winter Solstice feasting which Christmas replaced, have their origin in charity, benevolence and the common welfare of mankind. Being good, he suggests, is actually human nature. Modern, Christian life in 1843 needs to rediscover that ancient, genetic code of being good that is inherent in all of us, even someone as despicable as Scrooge.

This is part of the way Dickens re-invents Christmas, moving it beyond a simply Christian tradition celebrating Jesus's birth. To him, it is a celebration of mankind's goodness to fellow men, and the sheer joy of being alive.

Moral Duty to Educate the Poor

The ghost also leaves Scrooge with a moral message about society. He warns Scrooge of the "Doom" which is coming. Although unspecified, it suggests violent civil unrest if boys are left in "Ignorance". This is a plea for education, because educated boys are employable in better paid jobs. This will lift the poor out of poverty.

While the Malthusian solution to poverty is to "decrease the surplus population" by allowing them to "die" young from their poverty, the ghost offers an alternative. Society should "decrease the surplus population" by educating it, so that people are not "surplus," but essential. Educated people also have educated children, who then have useful jobs and are also not "surplus".

They are Man's…. And they cling to me, appealing from their fathers. The boy is Ignorance. The girl is Want. Beware of them both, and all of their degree, but most of all beware this boy, for on his brow I see that written which is Doom, unless the writing be erased.

This warning is well timed. Dickens was not making mad predictions here. Karl Marx was writing his Communist Manifesto at the same time, having seen the terrible consequences of inner-city poverty in England. He published it in February 1848. In Europe, the poor were beginning to protest, and in 1848, only five years after the novel, revolutions swept across the countries of Europe.

Dickens also subtly suggests that "Want" and "Ignorance" are actually created by businessmen like Scrooge. Remember how Scrooge was described in a list of seven adjectives, "a squeezing, wrenching, grasping, scraping, clutching, covetous, old sinner"? The child spirits are also described in a string of adjectives as "wretched, abject, frightful, hideous, miserable…Yellow, meagre, ragged, scowling, wolfish." This similarity invites the reader to ask how Scrooge and these children are linked, and the answer is, by cause and effect.

The Morality of Money Lending

Bank loans were very hard to come by if you were an ordinary citizen. You would need to visit a money lender, like Scrooge and Marley or, if they wouldn't lend you enough, take something you owned to a pawn broker. Some estimates show that there were nearly as many pawn brokers as pubs in Victorian Britain.

To Dickens, money lenders were symbols of evil, because of his family history. You are probably aware that his own father was sent to debtor's prison when Dickens was twelve. Dickens' mother forced him to quit school and work full time in a tanning factory, to support the family. Money lenders and pawn shops can only exist for two reasons. Poor people are too stupid to save, or they are too poor to save. In this book, Dickens argues that it is the second reason. This means he blames society, and the reader, for paying such low wages to the people who work for them.

He never blames Scrooge for charging too much interest.

Did you notice that when he visits a husband and wife who are thrilled that he has died (in Stave Four), they never complain about how much he is charging them (because it is the going rate for all money lenders)? Instead, they complain that he is "merciless" because he won't wait "a week" for his money when it is overdue.

So, Dickens' point is not just that Scrooge has built his wealth off the backs of poor people, but that this is how the readers are also maintaining their wealth - they simply pay their staff the going rate, which is too low. It is the reader's fault that the pawn brokers and the money lenders can grow rich.

An Entertaining Digression

To give you an insight in to how low wages were, here is a popular song from around 1850:

> "Half a pound of tuppenny rice,
> Half a pound of treacle,
> That's the way the money goes,
> Pop goes the weasel!"

To "pop" was to take an item to the pawn brokers, and the "weasel" was a shortening of "weasel and stoat", rhyming slang for coat. Stairs were "apples and pears", while my favourite, wife, was "trouble and strife". (Don't tell her I said that!)

Theme of Christmas Spirit

If we include the title, 'Christmas' is mentioned 86 times in this novel. Pretty much everything in the novel is connected to the Christmas spirit. You can link it to all of these;

- The charitable collections
- The hope for Tiny Tim
- The Cratchit family making a great celebration and feast out of poverty and a lack of food
- Scrooge's return to his family as a boy, and the boy singing Christmas carols.
- The many people from all levels of society whom the Ghost of Christmas Present shows to Scrooge.
- The generosity and love of celebration in Fezziwig's ball, and Fred's Christmas party.

Christmas time … a kind, forgiving, charitable, pleasant time; the only time … when men and women seem by one consent to open their shut-up hearts freely, and to think of people below them as if they really were fellow-passengers to the grave, and not another race of creatures bound on other journeys.

Fred

Dickens uses Fred as Scrooge's alter ego. They share much of the same genes, so Fred becomes a model of what Scrooge can become if he chooses (and at the end of the novel, he does).

He makes Fred complain about the one thing which is wrong with Dickens' readers, rather than what is wrong with Scrooge. Scrooge is a misanthrope, which means he dislikes everyone. If you are human, that is reason enough for Scrooge to dislike you.

Fred loves Christmas because, he argues, most people treat those who are socially inferior to them as not just "below them", but "another race of creatures". That's pretty extreme. He accuses Dickens' readers of behaving as though their house staff are not even fully human.

If Dickens's society was racist, Fred is arguing that the working classes and the poor are treated as though they come from "another race", of inferior people. Fred goes beyond that. He is suggesting that the treatment of the poor is much worse than racism, because it treats the poor as less than human, as "creatures".

The magic of Christmas is that it strips all this prejudice away, and everyone feels honest emotions - they "open their shut-up hearts freely" and become more truly human. To Dickens, Christmas doesn't just make us nicer, it reveals how good we really are. Society, and its hierarchy, is what harms everyone.

Just to make sure we understand that Fred is carrying Dickens's views, Bob Cratchit applauds this speech.

Grade 9 Context about Racism Because it is Cool to Know

The history of British colonialism is, to a modern audience, a violent, racist conquest. It is easy to imagine that Victorian Britain, when the Empire was at its strongest, was also a deeply racist society. Although by modern standards this is true, 1843 had seen amazing strides in politics to change the status of colonial peoples, and slavery in particular.

William Wilberforce became the first politician to campaign for the abolition of slavery in 1787. By 1807, The Slave Trade act stopped the trade in slavery in Britain, and in 1811 The Slave Trade Felony Act made it illegal in the Caribbean colonies. Between 1808 and 1860, the British navy freed 150,000 slaves by policing shipping on the African coast. In 1833 slavery was also prohibited in British colonies, and another 800,000 slaves were freed.

The last parts of the British colonies to allow slavery were territories controlled by The East India Company, which controlled India and Ceylon. The year when this slavery was outlawed: 1843, the same year Dickens wrote **A Christmas Carol**. So, it is very likely that Fred himself would not have seen himself as racist - through Fred, Dickens is pointing towards men being seen as equals (at least in the way that Victorians would have understood this).

Although it is tempting to look back on Victorians as unenlightened and cruel, it is helpful to know the economic value of what they gave up when banning slavery - it was valued at 16 billion pounds. This is the modern equivalent of what the government paid slave owners in compensation. So, the actual cost to the economy was 32 billion. That is a hell of a lot of money to give up in order to back a principle.

To put this in perspective, Britain is the second largest arms exporter in the world, with a trade worth *only* 11 billion per year. Incredibly, we also sell arms to nearly 80% of countries which face arms embargoes, (because their governments use the weapons on their own people).

And yet none of our political parties are campaigning for an end to this arms trade because, you know, money, money, money.

Theme of Winter and the Mythology of Christmas

Dickens also writes about Christmas as being so much better because it takes place in winter.

There was nothing very cheerful in the climate or the town and yet there was an air of cheerfulness abroad that the clearest summer air and brightest summer sun might have endeavoured to diffuse in vain.

When you think about it, this is a very bizarre description of Christmas. Yes, it spreads "cheerfulness". Yet Christmas is also better because it is not "clearest summer", but frozen winter.

In part this could be because general hardship forces people to be kinder to each other (remember the first Covid lockdown and the huge spread in volunteering, the celebration of the NHS?) It is also a celebration of winter, and points to Dickens' message that mankind's kindness to fellow men is ancient, part of human nature, and a tradition which predates Christianity. This link is made because Christmas replaced what was originally the Winter Solstice, celebrated for thousands of years before Christianity.

Dickens Adds to the Christmas Myth

[E]very man among them hummed a Christmas tune, or had a Christmas thought, or spoke below his breath to his companion of some by-gone Christmas Day, with homeward hopes belonging to it. And every man on board… had a kinder word for one another on that day than on any day in the year…

- Can you remember what book Dickens' stole Topper's blind man buff from?
- Which book did the Goblins feature in?

Dickens delivers his trademark sentimentalism here and it is easy to dismiss it as slightly sickening. I can't be the only one! But if it didn't contain some truth, no one would accept it. Dickens also wants to create a Christmas memory, a myth which his readers will return to every year.

You might think it is a bit of a stretch to think that Dickens planned this book as a reinvention of Christmas, so that he would convince his readers to think about Christmas differently forever. But actually, he had already experimented with stories about Christmas, and watched their impact on sales. In the **Pickwick Papers**, he had already published **"The Story of the Goblins Who Stole a Sexton"**, which included the prototype of the ghosts and Scrooge. The Cratchits' Christmas is nearly stolen entirely from an American author, Washington Irving, and his book **The Sketch Book of Geoffrey Crayon, Gent**.

The genius of Dickens' insight was in realising that Christmas sells. Better than that, it will keep selling every year. Imagine how this discovery would feel to a writer whose normal income depends on him writing new instalments every week, to books which might fall out of favour once finished. But **A Christmas Carol** could get reprinted every year: goldmine!

Christmas Traditions

Christmas tradition was based on rural communities, with Yuletide. Feasts would be of goat or boar, enough to feed several families, and often taking place outdoors. The family wouldn't sit around a coal fire, but would burn a Yule log, perhaps telling ghost stories. But in the forty years before **A Christmas Carol** was written a huge surge of population left the country to live in cities. London's population had doubled from 1 million to 2 million by 1850.

This urbanisation meant that Christmas traditions needed to be reinvented - an opportunity which Dickens took brilliantly. He was still trying to shape Christmas in a short story in 1850, beginning a short story with this line: **"I have been looking on, this evening, at a merry company of children assembled round that pretty German toy, a Christmas Tree."** We can see that Prince Albert was having success in introducing the Christmas tree (the Tannenbaum) from Germany, and how this tries to bring the Yuletide countryside setting into city life.

Dickens was even quick to spot the shift in feasting away from a goose to a turkey, a tradition he imported from America. This is why Scrooge buys a turkey **"twice the size of Tiny Tim"**, to emphasise how important this would be for poorer urban families - more protein for the same price.

In 1851 in his magazine Household Words, Dickens wrote about Christmas as a myth, as a truth which is not real, but operates like a shared memory:

> "That was the time for the bright visionary Christmases which have long arisen from us to show faintly, after summer rain, in the palest edges of the rainbow! *That was the time for the beatified enjoyment of the things that were to be, and never were, and yet the things that were so real in our resolute hope that it would be hard to say, now, what realities achieved since, have been stronger!*"

Theme of Family

We've seen that Fan is based on Dickens' older sister, Fanny. We've seen how Tiny Tim, and his vulnerability, are based on Fanny's son, Scrooge's nephew, Harry. Family is at the heart of his inspiration.

He gives the Cratchits his own childhood home in Bayham Street in Camden Town. It resonated with Dickens, because his family moved there when he was ten, and his father was already suffering from debt. Only two years later, his father John was jailed in debtors' prison, and Dickens was forced out to work. We can see that the Cratchit family are therefore on the brink, like his own family were - the slightest good fortune, like a giant turkey, can save a life, while the slightest misfortune can make a child's death much more likely.

We could argue that family is actually what saves Scrooge. Let's look at some evidence:

Fred says that he continually wishes Scrooge a happy Christmas every year, in the hope that this will lead to Scrooge paying Bob Cratchit more: **"If it only puts him in the vein to leave his poor clerk fifty pounds, that's something; and I think I shook him yesterday."** His family laughs to hear Fred's optimism, but at the end of the novel, this is exactly what happens.

Family is also at the root of Scrooge's pain. His childhood self has, as you know, been metaphorically abandoned by his dead mother, and literally abandoned by his father. Eventually Fan comes to rescue him from boarding school: **"Father is so much kinder than he used to be."** But she comes alone: Scrooge's father is still distant and aloof, and sends young Scrooge to be apprenticed to Fezziwig, where he also lodges. Scrooge's father simply doesn't want anything to do with him.

A Little More About Attachment Theory

Ok, take a moment to learn about this, it might change your life. We all reproduce the relationships we have in our first three years of life. This is very bad news if you didn't have great relationships with your immediate family and carers. Even worse, none of us can remember our first three years.

So, let's imagine you had an unloving relationship with a parent. You will actually seek out close relationships with people who are unloving. Of course, you won't know you are doing this, because you have no memory of your early years. You will just think you are attracted to someone for all sorts of other reasons. You won't know that all those emotional triggers deep in your brain are reacting to something completely different.

This is what is happening to poor old Scrooge. The older he gets, the more he seeks out relationships in which he will be rejected or abandoned.

The Role of the Father

We realise how important family is, and in particular the role of the father, when we see how this treatment so damages Scrooge. Write down what you know, and then test it against what I have written:

For his whole life, he is unable to escape this pattern, and repeats it in all his relationships. So, he treats Fred as his own father treated him. He picks a much younger woman, Belle, to be his fiancé, and then fails to show her enough affection so that this, combined with her youth, make it much more likely she will reject him.

He rejects any other woman, never seeking another relationship other than his partnership with Marley. This partnership is again like a marriage - they both live together. And similarly, he has chosen, in Marley, an older man, who will also one day abandon him, by dying earlier. Dickens' emphasises that the turning point in Scrooge's understanding happens in Stave Three, when he visits a fully functioning family, the Cratchits. But first, in Stave Two, the Ghost of Christmas Past forces him to see Belle's new family. Scrooge does not regret losing Belle's love as much as he regrets the loss of family, and not having a daughter: **"when he thought that such another creature, quite as graceful and as full of promise, might have called him father, and been a spring-time in the haggard winter of his life, his sight grew very dim indeed."**

Dickens' Family Context

Dickens' own children were a great disappointment to him, but this was all in the future in 1843. At this time, Dickens was considered a marvellous father, organising entertainments and plays starring all his children.

Later he complained of "having brought up the largest family ever known with the smallest disposition to do anything for themselves." He complained to one of his sons about another son, Sydney, who had amassed large debts: "I fear Sydney is much too far gone for recovery and I begin to wish that he were honestly dead." He did then die aged 25. His aunt, Georgina, who lived with Charles and his wife Catherine, brought the children up. She remarked of Sydney's death, "I fear we must feel that his being taken away early is the most merciful thing that could have happened to him, but it is very, very sad to have to feel this."

I include this because it does suggest Dickens himself wrestled with the idea of family. It was both incredibly important to him, but also an inconvenience. In 1857 he fell in love with an 18-year-old actress, Ellen Ternan, separated from his wife and kept Georgina at home with him to look after the children. In this way, Dickens seems to have been both like the reformed Scrooge, who became "a second father" to Tiny Tim, and like Scrooge's own father who treated his son with disdain.

The Cratchit Family

The Cratchits are symbolic of what Dickens wants us to value in a family. They rejoice in each other's hopes, and are relentlessly positive, no matter what the odds of failure or disaster. So:

- Peter **"rejoiced to find himself so gallantly attired"**, even though he is wearing his father's second hand, and totally out of fashion, shirt.

- Martha intends to hide from her father Bob on Christmas day, but **"Martha didn't like to see him disappointed, if it were only in joke"**.

- Tiny Tim views his disability as a "cripple" as a useful reminder to the congregation in church, to remind them of Jesus: **"it might be pleasant to them to remember upon Christmas Day, who made lame beggars walk, and blind men see."**

- Bob pretends to his wife that Tiny Tim is likely to recover, so his voice **"trembled more when he said that Tiny Tim was growing strong and hearty."**

- The Cratchits pretend that the goose is huge, but we find that they even had to eat the bones: **"surveying one small atom of a bone upon the dish"**.

- The pudding appears to be more "steam" than "flour", **"but nobody said or thought it was at all a small pudding for a large family. It would have been flat heresy to do so"**.

The Ending

Although the main message about Scrooge is that he has become a reformed employer, the main character development is that he has understood the meaning of family. This is why Dickens makes him a "second father" to Tiny Tim and why his first visit is to Fred and his family.

Theme of Redemption

Many readers struggle to believe that Scrooge could ever change into **"as good a friend, as good a master, and as good a man, as the good old city knew, or any other good old city, town, or borough, in the good old world"**.

After all, it was only yesterday (Christmas Eve) when Scrooge was **"a squeezing, wrenching, grasping, scraping, clutching, covetous, old sinner! Hard and sharp as flint"** and believed the poor should choose to "die" if they don't want to go to the workhouse.

But to them I say, Bah, Humbug.

Scrooge goes on a convincing psychological journey. This is one way to think about the journey the ghosts take him on - a journey of his psychological past, so that he can change his, and Tiny Tim's, future.

1. **Scrooge's Childhood:** The ghost of Christmas Past takes Scrooge back to his childhood. There was nothing miserly about him as a boy. The *only* reason to do this is to provide the psychological insight for how Scrooge grew up to be a misanthropic miser.

2. We find Scrooge abandoned at school over Christmas. We realise his mother is dead, and his father has abandoned him. This arrangement means he has also been abandoned by his friends, as they return home for Christmas: **"A solitary child, neglected by his friends, is left there still."**

3. **Fan's Love and Abandonment:** Then we return to the school some years later, to find that he is finally going to be allowed back home. However, his father still refuses to come. His sister Fan clearly loves him, but she too is forced to abandon him: "And you're to be a man!" said the child, opening her eyes, **"and are never to come back here; but first, we're to be together all the Christmas long, and have the merriest time in all the world."** Scrooge will become "a man" by being apprenticed to Fezziwig. So, "but first" tells us that Scrooge is only going to have one Christmas at home, and then be sent to live with Fezziwig.

4. Next Dickens wants us to know immediately that Fan abandons him very early, in death. We know she was young, because she has left only "one child". This now explains why Scrooge will not dare form an attachment to Fred, his nephew. He is a permanent reminder that whatever Scrooge loves is taken away from him. Far better to turn against mankind than to be endlessly tortured by loss.

5. **Belle's Love and Abandonment:** There is a real ambiguity in how his next love, Belle, abandons him. It is very easy to read her words about him loving another "idol", "profit", more than her as absolutely true. After all, we see him as an old man who seems to love nothing more than hoarding money.

   But we realise this desire to control is simply a fear of abandonment. Storing up love has had the opposite effect, and lead only to losing the people he loves. His money grows as he hoards, and no one can take it from him. We learned in Stave one that he has no interest in spending it on himself, barely using any coal in his fire, eating only "gruel" (the food of the workhouse).

6. **Belle's and Scrooge's Lost Family:** Scrooge realises that he has lost the chance of marriage and loving a woman. What motivates him next is seeing Belle's new family, and in particular a daughter:

"and when he thought that such another creature, quite as graceful and as full of promise, might have called him father, and been a spring-time in the haggard winter of his life, his sight grew very dim indeed."

He no longer looks enviously at Belle, his lost love, but at the "father" in the family scene, and his relationship with his daughter, who "might have called him father, and been a spring-time in the haggard winter of his life".

What is significant here is that he is already thinking about change now, "in the haggard winter of his life". He realises that becoming a father figure is the pivotal change which will make sense of his life, and erase his own father's influence. Becoming a father figure is going to be his true redemption.

7. **Tiny Tim is Scrooge's Turning Point:** When the Ghost of Christmas Present shows him the Cratchits' Christmas, his main concern is as a father figure: **"Spirit," said Scrooge, with an interest he had never felt before, "tell me if Tiny Tim will live."**

8. Dickens signals that this is a turning point by telling us that Scrooge had never had this interest in Tiny Tim before. It is because he is now thinking as a father. When we get to the end of the novel, Dickens gives the last words to Tiny Tim to emphasise how important he is to Scrooge's redemption.

9. The other way he signals this pivotal turning point is structural. It happens right in the middle of the novel, Stave Three. It suggests that everything we have seen so far has been leading up to this point, and that all the changes Scrooge makes after this point are caused by it.

10. This explains why, at the end, Dickens tells us Scrooge became "a second father" to Tiny Tim. Scrooge's redemption is based on realising that his own misanthropy started with his relationship with his own cold, distant and unloving father. Becoming a father figure himself allows him to right that wrong, and escape that pattern of attachment. Once he changes this fundamental relationship, he now loses his fear of abandonment, and can also begin to love his fellow man.

11. **Removing the Fear of Abandonment:** Another way in which this redemption is plausible is that Scrooge knows he won't be abandoned by Tiny Tim if he steps in to help. Whereas the ghost has told him that if he doesn't act, Tiny Tim will die. But if he helps, the abandonment stops, and Tiny Tim lives.

12. The ghost repeats a warning to Scrooge: **"If these shadows remain unaltered by the Future"**, Tiny Tim will die. But the repetition drums home to Scrooge that he can alter the future - his actions will therefore keep Tiny Tim alive. In other words, where all his

other loving relationships have ended in failure, Scrooge has a guarantee that this one will end in spectacular success. This completely removes his fear of abandonment.

13. **Scrooge's Redemption is Aimed at Society's Redemption:** The final clue that this redemption is psychologically convincing is the evidence the ghosts have presented around poverty and wages. This evidence has included:

    - "Ignorance and Want"
    - The charwoman, laundress and undertaker's man driven by poor wages to steal from Scrooge's corpse
    - The Cratchits desperate for work for Peter, and for enough food to keep their children alive

14. Through these, Scrooge has seen that the evil in society is not being a miser, but paying the going rate. He has realised that society itself is the problem, with its Malthusian dismissal of the poor as "idle" and "surplus", and its exploitation of a huge labour force by paying low wages.

    This is why Dickens also ends the novel with Scrooge giving Bob, not a charitable bonus, but an increase in salary: **"I'll raise your salary, and endeavour to assist your struggling family"**.

    Notice that the assistance to Bob's family goes beyond the salary - again, this is not charity, but a reference to employment, and in particular finding Peter a paid role.

15. In this way, Dickens links Scrooge's personal redemption to society's need to redeem itself.

Theme of Time

In my favourite book, **Slaughterhouse Five,** Billy Pilgrim "comes unstuck in time" and, without warning, can find himself transported to any moment in his life - past or future - to relive it. Kurt Vonnegut explores how we deal with tragedy, grief and hope through comedy, and this time-travelling plot device.

Well, Dickens does exactly the same in *A Christmas Carol*.

Time Running Out
The story begins with death: **"Marley was dead".**

The suggestion is that time is running out for Scrooge. He too will die, and he will suffer the kind of purgatory being suffered by Marley. The visit of Marley's ghost is a Memento mori - a device to remind a Christian that they must die. At this death, they will be judged by God, and so the reminder helps a Christian focus on doing good, leading a moral life, so their soul will go to heaven.

To a Christian, time is not the seventy odd years of life on the planet. Instead, it is an infinite experience for the soul. Life on earth is a tiny blip, **"a drop in the ocean"**, compared to an eternity in heaven or hell. A Christian has to ask themselves, what is a life well spent? What actions will lead to a soul going to heaven?

This explains Dickens' focus on the tormented ghost of Marley and that of the other ghostly businessmen who **"sought to interfere, for good, in human matters, and had lost the power for ever."** Because "human matters" only occur in the space of a human life, the most important measurement of time becomes a lifetime.

Dickens deliberately contrasts Scrooge's lifetime with Tiny Tim's. In the pivotal scene in the novella, Scrooge asks the Ghost of Christmas Present if Tiny Tim "will live", and the ghost replies that he will die before next Christmas. Dickens is using Tiny Tim as a symbol to represent all the unhealthy children of the poor. This asks the reader to consider that time is running out for the poor and disadvantaged, and in particular for their children.

This is exactly the kind of warning many charities use to ask us to donate. We can argue that this is exactly what Dickens does by introducing the charity collectors in Stave One. In Stave Five, Scrooge is transformed, and decides to pay a huge sum to charity, including "a great many back-payments".

Symbols of Time

Dickens scatters symbols of time, and time running out, throughout the novella. We might say it is obsessed with "time", a word which appears 84 times in the novella.

Bells: Stave One
In Stave One, the bells begin with a church.

"The ancient tower of a church, whose gruff old bell was always peeping slyly down at Scrooge out of a Gothic window."

This symbolises God's judgement on Scrooge's soul. The idea that God might be watching "slyly" is also a reminder that He sees everything, and every sin.

Next the bells become much louder (perhaps as an ironic reminder of how they might sound at the beginning of a sung Christmas carol). Here, they announce the arrival of Marley's ghost, and his warning to Scrooge.

"As he threw his head back in the chair, his glance happened to rest upon **a bell, a disused bell,** ... and with a strange, inexplicable dread, that as he looked, he saw **this bell begin to swing**. It swung so softly in the outset that it scarcely made a sound; but soon **it rang out loudly, and so did every bell in the house**.

This might have lasted half a minute, or a minute, but it seemed an hour. **The bells ceased as they had begun, together."**

Then Dickens decides that a **bell** must announce the arrival of each ghost of Christmas: "Without their visits," said the Ghost, "you cannot hope to shun the path I tread. Expect the first to-morrow, when the **bell tolls** One."

Bells: Stave Two
Although bells sound to announce the Ghost of Christmas Past, the most significant bells are in Scrooge's old school, and the name of his fiancé, Belle.

"They left the high-road, by a well-remembered lane, and soon approached a mansion of dull red brick, with a little weathercock-surmounted cupola, on the roof, and **a bell** hanging in it."

The school bell is always a reminder of each hour passing, announcing movement from one lesson to the next. But it also has the negative connotation of "hanging". Dickens suggests that the negative effects of time began when Scrooge was just a boy.

Belle
Remember how Belle was dressed "in a mourning dress" and how her name symbolised time running out?

Bells in Stave Five
However, in Stave Five, the transformation of Christmas, and of Scrooge, means that the bells no longer symbolise time running out and impending disaster. Instead, they are "**merry bells**" which make the day **"glorious! Glorious!"**

They no longer symbolise the theme of lost time, but time gained.

The Future, the Present and the Past
Dickens wants us to understand our lives as like a chain of cause and effect. He introduces this idea with Marley's ghost. A normal chain is just linear, forged "link by link". Instead,

Marley's is circular, worn like a belt, which is what "girded" means: **"I girded it on of my own free will"**.

The symbolism is also introduced through Belle, **"But if you were free to-day, to-morrow, yesterday, can even I believe that you would choose a dowerless girl"**? Here, the present, future and past are all bound up together, like a circle. This is also why they don't appear in order - past, present, and future. The point of the imagery is that you can revisit the past, present and future, and so change them. By revisiting his past, Scrooge learns to realise the damaging effect his father had on him, and is able to repair that damage in his choices.

This is the point of the journeys Scrooge makes with the ghosts, and why he says in Stave Four and repeats in Stave Five **"I will live in the Past, the Present, and the Future. The Spirits of all Three shall strive within me."** This linear structure of time is now much more like a circle - as all points seem to touch each other - they all "strive within" at the same time.

Why Do the Ghosts Arrive at One?

Dickens emphasises this point with the timing of each ghost. A logical timing might be to have them visit in sequence, midnight, one and two a.m. for example. But instead, Dickens insists they arrive at the same time on the same night. He means us to understand that the past, present and future exist in us *at the same time*.

This tells us that, like Scrooge, we can change our futures by revisiting our past. If we look at the most painful or significant moments in our past, we will find clues to our life choices. We can look back on these, as Scrooge does, and realise that we not only made the wrong choices, but also make new ones. We can return to a childhood state and become **"like a baby"**, just as Scrooge does.

Dickens emphasises the unity of time in another symbol. The logical time for Scrooge's haunting in **"A Ghost Story for Christmas"** would obviously be midnight. Instead, Dickens makes them arrive at "one". One is a symbol of unity, like our sense of self or identity. It is made up of the three parts - past, present and future - as we are made up of those. It is even, as a word, made up of three letters (though that may just be a coincidence).

Grade 9 Essays

1. How is A Christmas Carol a Criticism of Social Policy in Victorian England?

Dickens shows his opposition to The Poor Laws, which created **"workhouses"**, by making Scrooge support them: **"Are they still in operation?"**. Scrooge also supports the criminalisation of the poor, **"Are there no prisons?"** and believes these are necessary to **"decrease the surplus population"**, even if this means the poor would **"rather die"** than attend them. The Ghost of Christmas Present quotes Scrooge's support back at him ironically when Scrooge is desperate to save Tiny Tim, now that he knows what **"the surplus population"** looks like.

This language uses the politicians' interpretation of Thomas Malthus's economic theory. Because only male property holders could vote, Dickens targets his book at them, pricing it at an expensive five shillings, a third of the **"fifteen shillings"** a worker like Bob Cratchit earns. Dickens invites the readers into the warmth of the Cratchits' family Christmas, so that they too can understand the social effects of low wages.

On the way, Scrooge challenges the ghost for shutting bakers on a Sunday, which was a law upholding the Christian tradition of the Sabbath, forbidding trade, which will **"cramp these people's opportunities of innocent enjoyment...deprive them of their means of dining every seventh day"**. Dickens juxtaposes the harshness of society with the **"hard and sharp as flint"** Scrooge, pointing out that the miser is actually more generous than the reader who votes for such laws.

Inside the Cratchits' home on Christmas day, we wait for the eldest daughter Martha, a maid of all work, who has still had to **"clear away"** on Christmas morning for her thoughtless, and entirely normal, employers. The mother and second daughter make their old dresses appear more festive with **"ribbons"**, Peter wears a ridiculously large present of his father's old shirt, whose collar is so big it gets **"into his mouth"**. Only Bob and Tiny Tim have been to church, presumably because the rest of the family lack suitable clothing. Bob himself has no **"greatcoat"** and his best clothes are **"threadbare"**. Although this is a comic portrait, it is also a clue that the winter is a threat to health in a poor family.

Next, Dickens italicises the children's excitement at the feast: **"there's *such* a goose,"** and contrasts this with the goose's meagre size, so that the family even eat the bones, and there is only an **"atom of a bone"** left on the table. After witnessing this comic scene, Scrooge brings us back to real life, asking the Ghost **"if Tiny Tim will live"**. He won't.

So, Dickens challenges his readers to realise that the going rate of pay creates the working poor, which leads to their malnourishment, poor health, servitude and often death. Scrooge, like the reader, has simply supposed the poor are **"idle people"** who choose poverty because of defective character. Dickens wants to disabuse these readers, as he shocks Scrooge into transforming.

It is tempting to see Scrooge's transformation as needing The Ghost of Christmas Yet to Come, but actually this question in Stave Three is the pivotal moment. Dickens shows us this structurally, as it occurs in the middle of the novel, and also thematically at the end, when Scrooge becomes a **"second father"** to Tiny Tim.

If this last ghost is not necessary for Scrooge's transformation, why is he introduced? Dickens uses him to show the reader how wider society is affected by their poor pay. Bob has a comparatively good job for a working-class man. Those who earn less live in slums, where he now takes us: **"the whole quarter reeked with crime, with filth, and misery"**. Like the reader, Scrooge has avoided seeing the **"wretched"** conditions in which the poor live, and **"never penetrated"** there.

Here we meet tradespeople Scrooge has employed, a **"laundress"** and **"charwoman"**, and an **"undertaker's man"** who has prepared Scrooge's body. They have all stolen from the dead man's room. They have **"all three met here without meaning it!"** because they are embarrassed at their crimes. They are surprisingly polite to each other, and with **"gallantry"** decide that the poorest, the cleaner, should be last to ask old Joe for a price for her stolen goods, and therefore get a better price. Old Joe himself has made a tiny profit from crime. He is still having to do this, even though **"nearly seventy years of age"**. His poverty is introduced comically as he invites them into **"the parlour... the space behind the screen of rags."** This ironic juxtaposition reveals Dickens' social commentary, where not just poverty, but a significant amount of crime is caused by middle class indifference to the consequence of low wages which they pay.

This is harder for a modern audience to grasp, but all Dickens' original readers were exactly this kind of employer. Even Fred, the model of Christmas cheer who puts up with his uncle's **"Bah...Humbug!"** has a live-in housekeeper who is still working on Christmas day to welcome Scrooge to Fred's home. Dickens expects the reader to identify with the morally good **"master"** Fred and perhaps now to question their indifference to the lives of their employees.

Dickens also warns of greater consequences than crime if society, and the reader, does not change. Because Scrooge begins his transformation, he notices the figures of **"Ignorance"** and **"Want"** whom Dickens personifies as a boy and a girl. The Ghost of Christmas Present delivers Dickens' warning, **"but most of all beware this boy, for on his brow I see that written which is Doom, unless the writing be erased." "Ignorance"** symbolises the lack of education denied to the poor, which results in a spiral of unemployability, or a qualification only for low-wage work. This unspecified **"doom"** suggests violent crime or political protest, or perhaps predicts the kinds of revolution which swept Europe five years later.

This scene is not necessary to the plot of Scrooge's redemption, so it works like an aside to the reader, calling our attention to the author's wider purpose, which is not just to entertain, but persuade the reader to build a fairer society.

Therefore, Dickens ends the novella with Scrooge raising Bob's **"salary"** as his final act. We remember that his lack of charity was a sign of his miserly behaviour. But Bob's salary was only the going rate in 1843, not a product of Scrooge's miserliness. So, this action becomes a clear signal to the reader to increase what they pay their employees and domestic staff. The final line, ending with **"God bless us"** is partly ironic. God isn't going to help the poor, so we, like Scrooge, have to.

Rewritten as an Exam Answer

How is A Christmas Carol a Criticism of Social Policy in Victorian England?

Although Dickens writes the novel as an entertainment, he wants the story of Scrooge's moral awakening to "haunt" the reader, and so lead to a change in how his readers think about the poor.

Dickens shows his opposition to The Poor Laws, which created **"workhouses"**, by making Scrooge support them: **"Are they still in operation?"**. Scrooge also supports the criminalisation of the poor, **"Are there no prisons?"** and believes these are necessary to **"decrease the surplus population"**. Then Dickens creates Tiny Tim to show us what **"the surplus population"** looks like, and he uses Tiny Tim's impending death to transform Scrooge's view.

Scrooge's words refer to Thomas Malthus's economic theory and the cruelty of social policy. Because only male property holders could vote, Dickens targets his book at them, pricing it at an expensive five shillings, a third of the **"fifteen shillings"** a worker like Bob Cratchit earns. Dickens invites these readers, who would employ domestic servants, into the warmth of the Cratchits' family Christmas, so that they too can understand the social effects of low wages.

On the way, Scrooge challenges the ghost for shutting bakers on a Sunday, which actually attack the poor, and "**deprive [s] them of their means of dining every seventh day**". Dickens juxtaposes the harshness of society with the **"hard and sharp as flint"** Scrooge, to point out that the miser is actually more generous than the reader who votes for such laws.

Cratchit's daughter Martha, a domestic servant, has still had to **"clear up"** on Christmas morning for her thoughtless, and entirely normal, employers. Mrs Cratchit has tried to make old dresses appear more festive with **"ribbons"**; Peter wears a ridiculously, out of fashion, second hand shirt, whose collar is so big it gets **"into his mouth"**. Only Bob and Tiny Tim have been to church, presumably because the rest of the family lack suitable clothing. Bob himself has no **"greatcoat"** and his best clothes are **"threadbare"**. Although this is a comic portrait, it is also a clue that the winter is a threat to health in a poor family and a threat to their Christianity.

Next, Dickens italicises the children's excitement at the feast: **"there's *such* a goose,"** and contrasts this with the goose's meagre size. The starving family even eat the bones, so there is only an **"atom of a bone"** left. After witnessing this comic scene, Scrooge brings us back to real life, asking the Ghost **"if Tiny Tim will live"**. He won't.

So, Dickens challenges his readers to realise that the going rate of pay creates the working poor, which leads to their malnourishment, poor health, and often death. Scrooge, like the reader, has simply supposed the poor are **"idle people"** who choose poverty because of defective character. Dickens challenges these readers, as he shocks Scrooge into transforming.

Scrooge's transformation can happen right here, in Stave Three, where Scrooge decides he needs to save Tiny Tim. Dickens points this out to us at the end, when Scrooge becomes a **"second father"** to Tiny Tim. So, this poses a question. If this last ghost is not necessary for Scrooge's transformation, why is he introduced?

Dickens uses him to show the reader how wider society is affected by their poor pay. Those who earn less than Bob live in slums, where Dickens now takes us: **"the whole quarter reeked with crime, with filth, and misery"**.

Here we meet tradespeople Scrooge has employed, a **"laundress"** and **"charwoman"**, and an **"undertaker's man"**. They have all stolen from the dead man's room. They have **"all three met here without meaning it!"** because they are embarrassed at their crimes. They are surprisingly polite to each other, acting with **"gallantry"** to suggest that criminals are not evil, but driven to crime by poverty. Old Joe himself has made a tiny profit from crime. He is still having to do this, even though **"nearly seventy years of age"**. His **"parlour"** is only **"the space behind the screen of rags."** Dickens' lesson is that a significant amount of crime is caused by middle class indifference to the consequence of low wages which they pay.

Even Fred, the model of Christmas cheer who puts up with his uncle's **"Bah...Humbug!"** has a live-in housekeeper who is still working on Christmas day to welcome Scrooge to Fred's home. Dickens expects the reader to identify with the morally good **"master"** Fred and perhaps now to question their indifference to the lives of their employees.

This political message also explains the presence **"Ignorance"** and **"Want"**. Like the reader, Scrooge cannot see them, until he has started to transform. Dickens personifies them as a boy and a girl. The Ghost of Christmas Present delivers Dickens' warning, **"but most of all beware this boy, for on his brow I see that written which is Doom, unless the writing be erased."** **"Ignorance"** symbolises the poor are refused. This will in unqualified, low paid workers, or unemployment, which will cause **"doom"**. Perhaps this will be violent crime, political protest, or even predicts the kinds of revolution which swept Europe in 1848.

This scene calls our attention to the author's wider purpose, to persuade us to build a fairer society.

Therefore, Dickens ends with Scrooge raising Bob's **"salary"**. Bob's salary was only the going rate in 1843, not a product of Scrooge's miserliness. So, this action becomes a clear signal to the reader to increase what they pay their employees and domestic staff. The final line, ending with **"God bless us"** is partly ironic. God isn't going to help the poor, so we, like Scrooge, have to.

930 words

2. How Does Dickens Use the Ghosts in A Christmas Carol?

Dickens uses his ghosts in three ways. Firstly, to entertain with a traditional Christmas ghost story. Secondly to change tragedy into comedy, to resolve conflict in Scrooge's personal journey of redemption. And thirdly to educate readers about the need for social change which will lead to happy resolutions to the social conflicts of unemployment, poverty and lack of education.

The first ghost mentioned is that of **"Hamlet's Father"**, to suggest that Scrooge's story begins as a tragedy. This ghost is trapped in Purgatory, desperate for his son Hamlet to seek revenge. Dickens contrasts this with Marley's ghost, presented as a father figure to Scrooge. He tells Scrooge that he has intervened to help him redeem himself and escape Purgatory, with **"A chance and hope of my procuring, Ebenezer."** He wants Scrooge to become a benefactor to others, to improve the present and future of the poor and working poor.

Although this feels like a Christian message, encouraging Scrooge to think about the future and **"penance"** of his own soul, as the novel unfolds we find that Scrooge is much more motivated by helping others for the benefits they will receive now, in life, rather than gaining the eternal salvation. Although Marley is concerned with **"my fate"**, Scrooge is not interested in the **"fate"** of his soul, but the fate of the living.

The next ghosts he introduces are those of businessmen and **"guilty governments"** who are also in Purgatory because they can no longer help those in need. This is an overt political and social message, demanding that his affluent readers, who would own property and therefore have a right to vote in 1843, introduce laws which will reduce poverty, and pay higher wages.

Dickens contrasts this social duty with the laws at the time, which after 1834 forced the unemployed poor to work in prison-like **"workhouses"**. He suggests that these conditions will lead to despair and death by making one of the charity collectors suggest that **"many would rather die"** than live in them. Scrooge replies with the Malthusian justification that society needs to **"reduce the surplus population"**, and Dickens discredits this view by giving it to his villain.

The ghost carries Dickens' message that this **"surplus"** will be reduced if the population is educated and employed on fair wages. They would then become essential to the economy, rather than **"surplus"** to it. But to make Scrooge's transformation convincing, Dickens must show us Scrooge's formative childhood.

The Ghost of Christmas Past helps deliver the psychological basis for Scrooge's misanthropy, showing us how he was abandoned by his father as a **"forgotten boy"**. However, this ghost also has a social purpose, showing how the abandoned Scrooge is saved by his education. Consequently, fictional characters like **"Ali Baba"** and **"Robin Crusoe"** literally come to life as real figures in Scrooge's memory.

This ghost also shows Scrooge the importance of family when he sees the children he could have had with Belle. Dickens uses this to explain Scrooge's eventual transformation, when Scrooge understands he needs to become a **"second father"** to Tiny Tim and erase the cruelty of his own father. When Scrooge pictures a daughter, who **"might have called him father,**

and been a spring-time in the haggard winter of his life" he begs the ghost to stop, and physically attacks him.

This psychological journey is also symbolic. Dickens suggests that society needs to become a father, helping the poor rather than condemning them as **"idle"** and **"surplus"**.

The Ghost of Christmas present also uses Scrooge's Malthusian views satirically, quoting them back at Scrooge when he first starts to wonder how to improve the lives of the poor. As Scrooge transforms, he is able to notice the child spirits **"Ignorance"** and **"Want"**. The ghost warns Scrooge that ignorance is the most dangerous, bringing **"doom"**, because Dickens is warning society of the need to educate its children out of poverty, or face social and political unrest.

*Dickens also uses this ghost to emphasise the need for social cohesion. He portrays Christmas as a time when men are much kinder to each other. This ghost **"sprinkled incense"** which magically defuses conflict.*

*Dickens deliberately portrays him as a pagan figure, **"bare"** chested, in a **"green robe"**. Readers would associate him with the traditions of the winter solstice which pre-date Christianity. In other words, Dickens emphasises that mankind's instinct to be kinder to each other during the darkest parts of the year is the natural order, and not something men need to be taught through Christian teaching.*

This contrasts with the unjust Poor Laws passed by educated Christians, and with the low wages paid by churchgoing employers. It is worth knowing that Dickens priced this novel at five shillings, expensive enough so that only middle and upper-class readers could afford it. All such Victorian readers would have been employers of domestic staff, and spent a good deal on the service economy. They would all pay the going rate, which Dickens points out to us by always mentioning the precise salaries his working characters earn.

The Ghost of Christmas Yet to Come appears to contradict the importance of Dickens' social message by focusing on Scrooge's own personal journey. The spirit is **"shrouded in a deep black garment"** and these allusions to death act as a Memento Mori. Christian readers would see this as a didactic message, asking Scrooge to redeem his soul by reforming.

However, closer reading suggests this is not the ghost's main purpose. Dickens makes this **"phantom"** take Scrooge to London's slums, which **"reeked with crime, with filth, and misery."** He meets the charwoman, laundress and the undertaker's man, whose wages are so poor that they are driven to steal from Scrooge's corpse. Although the scene is comically macabre, and appears to condemn these ghoulish thieves, we are actually struck by their **"gallantry"** to each other. Dickens suggests that these are good people who have been forced into crime in order to survive.

Dickens contrasts them with the Cratchits who are good people, resist turning to crime, and regularly go to church. They live in hope that Peter will find employment and **"Tiny Tim will live"**. But the ghost reveals their moral behaviour doesn't prevent Tiny Tim from dying. Only food can do that, as we find out in Stave Five.

At the end of the novel the ghostly narrator decides that the most important lesson is about **"Tiny Tim, who did not die"**. This emphasises the importance of Scrooge's understanding of his role in becoming **"a second father"** to Tiny Tim. Symbolically, it emphasises how society needs to become a father to its own vulnerable population.

1103 words

You could leave out the paragraphs in italics under exam conditions - these total 178 words, leaving 925 words.

3. What is the Importance of Family in A Christmas Carol?

Although Christmas celebrations centre around the family, and Dickens offers us some brilliant comic set pieces with the Cratchits and Fred's family, at the heart of every family interaction is the role of the father. In a patriarchal society, Dickens explores male paternal behaviour as the most important relationship in society. This is why the novel ends with Scrooge becoming **"a second father"** to Tiny Tim. We know Dickens wanted his readers to appreciate this, as he deliberately rewrote the ending to include this in his final draft.

He also begins the novel with a father, the ghost of Hamlet's father, who begins his son's tragedy. Dickens playfully compares **"Old Marley"** to **"Hamlet's ghost"**, which portrays him as a father figure to Scrooge. We realise that this has been the most significant relationship in Scrooge's life as an adult. He keeps Marley's name above his business and happily answers when people call him Marley.

The importance of fatherhood is emphasised when Dickens shows us Scrooge's childhood, abandoned, **"solitary...neglected"** at school by an unloving father.

These references signpost abandonment as the dominant theme in Scrooge's psychological journey from the imaginative child who is friends with fictional characters **"Ali Baba"** and **"Robin Crusoe"**, to misanthropic miser.

Dickens introduces Fred, Scrooge's only relative, and the son of his beloved sister Fan, to show how damaged Scrooge is by his misanthropy, and avoidance of his own family. However, Fred's continued good cheer with Scrooge: **"why cannot we be friends?"** is not used to show the importance of family. Instead he wants to teach Scrooge to help his employee, Bob Cratchit: **"to leave his poor clerk fifty pounds"**. Dickens therefore suggests an employer is like a father figure, and consequently Scrooge's role is to look out for the well-being of Bob and his family by the end of the book.

Dickens emphasises this paternal role in his portrayal of Fezziwig, and Scrooge's deep appreciation of the role he played in bringing happiness to his surrogate children, **"the apprentices"** who slept on the premises for the seven years of their apprenticeship. Dickens points out **"He has the power to render us happy or unhappy"**.

The other paternal role played by employers is in paying higher wages - which Dickens highlights as an important theme when he makes Scrooge focus on increasing Bob's **"salary"** even when this is above the going rate (which Dickens' readers would quickly infer, as he is deliberate in stating Bob's original salary three times, at **"fifteen"** shillings).

Scrooge's sister, Fan, becomes important as a symbol of Scrooge's abandonment. Like Scrooge's mother, Fan dies young. This and Scrooge's father create Scrooge's pattern of attachment, choosing future relationships which will also inevitably lead to abandonment: he gets engaged to the much younger Belle, and he chooses as a business partner the much older **"Old Marley"**.

Scrooge can only escape this pattern, and his misanthropy, when he realises that he too can become a father. The ghost of Christmas past plants the seed of this idea when he shows Scrooge the daughter he never had, and Scrooge laments how Belle's daughter could have **"been a spring-time in the haggard winter of his life"**. This imagery of the seasons also suggests fatherhood is an essential natural experience.

He is taught how to be a father by his visit to the Cratchits, when he sees Bob literally and metaphorically lifting up Tiny Tim, and asks **"if Tiny Tim will live?"** When the ghost of Christmas Present looks into the future, Dickens effectively breaks the fourth wall of his universe because this should be the role of the Ghost of Christmas Yet to Come. This happens in Stave Three, a structural feature which Dickens uses as the pivotal moment of Scrooge's transformation. From now on, Scrooge is determined to change the future, not for the salvation of his own soul, but in order to transform the fortunes of others who become his surrogate family, and of Tiny Tim to whom he becomes **"a second father"**.

Dickens' circumstances, facing the birth of a fifth child, and feeling the financial pressures of sluggish sales of his previous two novels, are easily reflected in the poverty of the six-child Cratchit family. A further clue that we should make this connection with Dickens' role as a father is the fact that the Cratchits live in Dickens' own childhood home in **"Camden Town"**. His father moved there because of his own rising debts, and from here he was sent, along with his family, to debtors' prison. We can easily imagine Scrooge's redemption is also a rewriting of Dickens' own personal history, examining the role of his own father and vowing to make a better job of it by making a financial success of this novella.

Dickens makes Scrooge reclaim his family by attending Fred's **"Wonderful party"**, and enjoy Fred's paternal role in matchmaking for his niece. Again, the father's role is cast as benefactor, providing security and happiness for the family, as well as helping them to fall **"in love"** as he did.

Dickens also gives Scrooge the word **"love"** for the first time in the novel, with the knocker which had transformed into Marely's face, **"I shall love it, as long as I live!"** This again emphasises Marley's role as the father who has become his benefactor, enlisting the help of the three ghosts of Christmas to teach Scrooge to redeem himself by becoming **"a second father"** to Tiny Tim.

908 words

4. What is the Importance of Childhood in the Novel?

Following his visits to Cornish tin mines and factories in Manchester, Dickens was determined to change government policy on childhood poverty, education and employment. He had intended to write a pamphlet which would force political change, until the poor sales of his recent novels forced him to write something commercial. However, we can see Dickens' concerns and hopes about childhood reflected in the novel.

Dickens portrays childhood as the magical home of imagination, even in adversity. This is why the young abandoned schoolboy, Scrooge, so enjoys the fantasy of fiction that **"Ali Baba"** literally **"did come"** to life outside his school room window. Dickens deliberately chose a recent children's classic in order to emphasise the importance of literacy, not just for its educational benefit, but for its liberation of the imagination.

Through the young Scrooge, he also emphasises the importance of friendship when the old Scrooge **"knew and named them every one"** of the boys he passes with the ghost.

Children are also idealised, and contrasted to more wicked adults. Fan reacts to her father's newfound kindness, **"Father is so much kinder than he used to be"**, by asking him to bring the abandoned Scrooge home for a family Christmas, before he is apprenticed to Fezziwig. Tiny Tim also exhibits this kind of wisdom when he is delighted to attend church and be visibly noticed as **"a cripple"**, because it will remind the congregation of Jesus who made **"lame beggars walk and blind men see."**

To a Victorian reader, child mortality made the love of a child a mixed blessing. In 1843, between 30 and 50% of children died before the age of five. Fan dies as a young mother and Tiny Tim dies as a young boy. This is why Dickens has Bob Cratchit use Tiny Tim, and the family's love for him, as a way to teach Stoic acceptance, remembering **"how patient and how mild"** he was. Although this feels like an idealised, overly sentimental portrait, to Dickens' readers this would feel like a practical solution to a horrifyingly commonplace tragedy, the death of a child.

We can see that childhood is literally at the centre of the novel when we notice Scrooge's original transformation in Stave Three, where he asks the ghost of Christmas present **"if Tiny Tim will live"**. Dickens makes sure we understand it is this moment that changes Scrooge's misanthropy and miserliness, by returning to it in the final lines of the novel, and reminding us that Scrooge became **"a second father"** to Tiny Tim.

We can also sense Dickens' unhappiness with the middle-class habit of sending boys away to school, while educating girls at home. Instead of simply presenting Scrooge's father as cruel, Dickens emphasises the particular form of cruelty where a parent sends a child away to school. The young Scrooge is described as a **"solitary child"** and **"alone"**. The Ghost of Christmas Past takes Scrooge to his childhood so that he can learn how his misanthropy and miserliness grew - the child is the father to the man. So, we begin to understand that Scrooge pushes people away, because he is repeating the experience of being abandoned as a child. He worships the "idol" of money, because money can be hoarded and controlled, and will never abandon him if he refuses to spend it. Structuring the novel this way invites the reader to examine their own childhoods as the cause of their own character flaws.

Dickens also uses children to deal with the twin social dangers of poverty and lack of education. He creates the child spirits of "**Ignorance**" and **"Want"**. These dehumanised **"Yellow, meagre, ragged, scowling, wolfish"** figures are also warnings of what the present, 1843, will lead to in the future. Dickens is making a political point. What a society inflicts on its young people will return in opposition when these children grow into adults. This is why the ghost warns that **"ignorance"** is the child which will grow up to be society's **"doom"**. This is a warning of crime, civil unrest, and revolution, and foreshadows the actual European revolutions of 1848.

Although these spirits feel like an unnecessary addition to the tale, having no role in Scrooge's transformation, Dickens uses this scene to emphasise that society's treatment of its children is uppermost in the author's mind. He asks the reader to look at the ending, when Scrooge becomes **"a second father"** to Tiny Tim and a better employer to Bob Cratchit. We know this doesn't just complete his psychological journey, it is also a symbol of how a society should be the father to all its children. Even more important than alleviating poverty is the need to tackle the causes of poverty. So, Dickens proposes that removing a child's ignorance, through education, will give them the best chance of finding future employment. This role of the wealthy to become father figures to the working poor might be the **"Ghost of an Idea"** he hopes will **"haunt"** his readers.

830 words

5. How does Dickens use Fred to Explore Aspects of Victorian Society?

Dickens presents Fred as an idealised version of masculinity. Fred is portrayed as the ideal provider in a patriarchal society. He also does this with grace and a sense of humour, as Dickens uses him to demonstrate ideal masculine behaviour. He uses Fred to explore the importance of male role models in shaping character. Finally, Fred carries Dickens' message that the middle classes and upper classes need to raise the wages of their many employees and tradespeople.

We first meet Fred as an optimist, returning to his uncle Scrooge every Christmas, to wish him a **"merry Christmas"**, no matter how frequently or angrily he is rejected.

Here Dickens' social message centres around persistence. Fred's character implies that if you want to change the way people behave towards each other in society, you must persevere **"year after year"**. He invites us to **"laugh"** at Fred's optimism, as his family does when he tells them **"I think I shook him yesterday"**. He hopes Scrooge will give Bob **"fifty pounds,"** which amuses everyone. Yet Dickens emphasises Fred's importance when Scrooge does raise Bob's salary and attends Fred's party.

Dickens uses Fred to explore the plight of the working poor, represented by Bob Cratchit and his children. They are also forced to work in menial jobs like Martha, or search desperately for work, like the unemployed Peter. Fred's hope for **"fifty pounds"**. This is an enormous sum compared to the wages he is actually paid, of **"fifteen"** shillings a week, so it would take 66 weeks to earn this much. Dickens names this precise sum because he is pointing out how much money middle class employers could spare, and also to reveal the actual shortfall in a living wage for a married man with several children. Fred is putting forward Dickens' view that basic wages ought to be doubled.

Dickens makes sure that we understand these are not the unrealistic views of a young man. For this reason, he makes sure that Fred has a maid of all work as a live-in servant. It is clear that he knows the value of service. He pays well enough that she is actually working on Christmas Day, and is probably also invited to the family festivities.

The narrator also pretends to be shocked at the way Fred plays his patriarchal role so well. He is not content merely to be happily married, but takes on the responsibility of finding suitable husbands for his sisters in law. Dickens describes a game of blindman's buff which is rigged, "a done thing" so Fred's friend Topper court's the **"plump sister"**. Although the scene is presented as a pastiche of sensual seduction, with Topper and the plump sister eventually hiding **"behind the curtains"**, Fred has ensured that no scandal can be attracted to the romance, because it happens before witnesses. Consequently, the narrator makes sure to tell us The Ghost of Christmas Present also **"knew it"** and approved. Topper must also prove his serious intentions by paying handsomely for a **"ring"** and **"chain"**. In other words, Fred ensures that any suitors for his sisters in law are not only honourable in their intentions, but also affluent enough to provide them with secure lives. To Victorians, Fred is the model head of family in a patriarchal society. It is also important that there is no trace of arrogance or dominance in this role. Instead, Fred allows himself to be the butt of the women's jokes. His wife announces to everyone, "He is such a ridiculous fellow!", and everyone seems to agree. Fred, however, **"encouraged them in their merriment, and passed the bottle joyously."** (Here Dickens also uses Fred to attack the popular abstinence movement. It is a joke he returns to at the end when Scrooge does adopt the **"Total Abstinence Principle"** in his rejection of **"Spirits"**.)

Dickens makes the Ghost of Christmas Present bring Scrooge to this scene so that he can learn his lesson, not just about the joys of family life, and the pleasures that Christmas can offer, but to see a man's proper role as improving the lives of others, especially those who depend on him. Scrooge takes this lesson to heart when he decides to become a benefactor to Bob's family, and **"a second father"** to Tiny Tim. He also learns Fred's lesson about wages by insisting on increasing Bob Cratchit's salary. Dickens wants his readers to know that charity is desirable, but uses Fred to teach that raising wages is essential. The former will help, but the latter will transform family life and, as we see with the change of fate to Tiny Tim, can literally be the difference between life and death.

778 words

6. What are Dickens's Messages in A Christmas Carol?

Dickens has four main messages in **A Christmas Carol**. The first is to create the mythical power of Christmas, so that readers might celebrate it every year, and perhaps create a market for his book. He also wanted social change, so that his readers would reject the Malthusian justification for workhouses, and the criminalisation of the poor with prisons. However, he sees a much wider problem of poverty in the low wages that the middle and upper classes pay, and wishes to change his readers' habits as employers. Finally, he uses Scrooge's redemption to explore the psychological difficulties readers might have in changing, so that they too might overcome these as Scrooge does.

Dickens wrote **A Christmas Carol** over a period of six weeks, urgently needing financial success following poor sales of his previous two novels Barnaby Rudge and Martin Chuzzlewit, and an expensive tour to America. Mythologizing Christmas, and releasing the book on the 19th of December, would provide a synergy of timing and goodwill which he hoped would boost sales, and sell out the first 5000 print run.

To make this myth attractive, the setting is a much colder winter than those of the 1840s, harking back to the big freezes of previous decades. This element of nostalgia also created a branding of Christmas associated with **"snow"**, **"fog"** and **"cold"**. This helped him emphasise the contrast of warmth indoors which is mirrored in the warmth of family and friends in the portraits of Bob Cratchit's, Belle's and Fred's family gatherings.

He celebrates this further in Stave Three, through the journey Scrooge undertakes with the Ghost of Christmas Present. This spirit shows him lighthouse keepers, fisherman, miners, carefully chosen to represent the four elements of nature: fire, water, earth, with air being represented by his own flight with the spirit. These men in elemental settings, all sharing Christmas warmth and good cheer, suggest Christmas celebration is a force of nature. This also explains why he decides the Ghost of Christmas Present is a pagan figure, his **"green robe"** and **"bare"** chest reminding us of the Green Man. Dickens implies this winter fellowship, celebrating the Winter Solstice, is as **"joyful"** as the spirit, predating Christianity and therefore being a part of human nature.

Another ancient winter tradition is the ghost story, which Dickens makes into a Christmas tradition. Ghost stories were performed or read out loud. We can see this is planned for in Dickens' sentences: those overloaded with lists and adjectives; the many conversational exchanges where characters repeat themselves in order to create distinctive voices for a reader to mimic, and in the creation of a narrator obsessed with food and attractive women. This is the novel Dickens performed most in public, and its theme of Christmas ensured that a new market would be available every single year.

Beneath this celebration, Dickens attacks the Malthusian justification for workhouses, which criminalised the **"idle"** poor. So, he gives this view, that society should **"decrease the surplus population"** to his villain, the misanthropic Scrooge. He then attacks the view vigorously as Scrooge begins to see the terrible effects of poverty, and the ghost of Christmas present recites his own Malthusian words back at him. This ghost also brings the figures of

"Ignorance" and **"Want"** to show the dangers of not educating the poor by calling this mankind's **"doom"**. Dickens suggests that civil unrest and violence might well follow if his readers do not learn the lesson of his story and fail to prevent the injustices of child labour, illiteracy, low wages and unemployment.

He dramatises the hardships of the working poor through the Cratchits struggling on **"fifteen"** shillings per week, and of the working scavengers who profit from Scrooge's death by stealing from his corpse. We can see from the description of aged **"Old Joe"** and his **"parlour"** that crime pays very little but is necessary to supplement the terrible earnings of these serving staff. Dickens contrasts this to Bob Cratchit, who behaves in entirely moral and Christian ways, putting up with his poor wages and living on hope. The result of this, however, is that his son Tiny Tim dies from the effects of a poor diet. In contrast the immoral scavengers survive because, Dickens suggests, they are forced to become criminals. Dickens actually portrays them behaving with **"gallantry"**, firstly as a comic reversal of expectations, but secondly suggesting that they are not naturally disposed to evil and crime, but are driven to it by the poor wages his readers pay to such service staff.

This also explains why Dickens priced the book as a luxury item, at five shillings. He is targeting readers who own property, and therefore have a vote and can reject Malthusian politics. He also wants them to contrast the price to the mere **"fifteen"** shillings which Bob Cratchit receives, so they can appreciate how little they pay their own employees. Remember, Scrooge pays Bob the going rate, which is why he doesn't simply leave. Dickens dramatises this further at the end when he decides to **"raise [Bob's] salary"** and the reaction of others is to have **"their fill of laughter"** because he is seen as stupid for paying more than he has to.

All his readers, given the high price of the book, would have been employers of domestic servants and tradespeople, and this ending asks them whether they should be paying more, not just at Christmas, but through increased wages which will change lives or, like Tiny Tim's, save them.

914 words

7. How does Dickens Use Atmosphere and Setting?

Dickens *is very specific in his setting of **a Christmas Carol**. He* chooses London, because he knows his first readers will be middle and upper-class Londoners. He doesn't just want them to recognise the settings of Cornhill and Camden Town, he also wants them to feel that the characters, and in particular their poverty, live close by.

Because he is writing the novel in six weeks, in order to meet the deadline of Christmas itself, Dickens also realises the power of mythology around Christmas. He hopes to describe a Christmas which will always be true in the reader's imagination.

Consequently, *in Stave One*, the **"fog"** of London is accompanied by the **"cold"**, and **"frosty rime"** on Scrooge's **"head"**. He is like a personification of winter, and **"carried his own low temperature always about with him"**. **"No warmth could warm"** him, which works as a pathetic fallacy, telling the reader how cold-hearted Scrooge is. The metaphor of this setting also suggests that Scrooge is unnatural, so that even the changing seasons won't change his coldness.

The weather is unlike the Christmases of 1839 to 1843. Instead their extreme cold harks back *to the Christmases of 1837 to 38 and even further,* to the big freeze of 1813 to 1816 *when winter was so severe it was possible to hold a fair on the frozen river Thames. This is why the narrator begins with **"once upon a time"**.* When Dickens takes Scrooge back to his childhood, he deliberately introduces **"snow"**, equating it with Christmas and joy. By the end, this is also coupled with perfect sunshine, **"Golden sunlight; Heavenly sky"** which again, in a pathetic fallacy, mimics Scrooge's transformation.

Dickens understood that mythologising Christmas in this way, in its frozen snowy setting, would act as a kind of brand, and help his readers always associate a snowy winter with his novel. This would mean he could reprint it every winter and notice a surge in sales. *This was a new business model for him, and turned out to be incredibly successful. However, it is not an accident.* Dickens had already experimented with similar characters and settings in *The Pickwick Papers*, and even stole the scene with Topper directly from a previous best seller, Washington Irving's ***The Sketch Book of Geoffrey Crayon***.

Another winter tradition which Dickens exploits is the ghost story. Setting the plot in **"bleak...foggy"** weather allows him to characterise the houses as **"phantoms"**, and this foreshadows the ghosts which haunt Scrooge.

Although the ghost story and Christmas setting are the two hooks he uses to draw readers in *on the 19th of December, 1843,* Dickens also has the wider purpose of social reform. Consequently, *Dickens is particular about two addresses*. The Cratchits live in **"Camden Town"**, which Londoners would realise *was about three miles from the centre of London, where Scrooge has his offices at **"Cornhill"**. Readers would understand the address* was a place where poorer families would live and make do. However, *he chooses a particular house:* the Cratchits live in the same house Dickens' family occupied, as their fortunes declined and Dickens' father's debts mounted. It was from here that his father and family were taken to debtors' prison, and the 12-year-old Charles Dickens was sent to work in Warren's Blacking Factory to help pay off his father's debts.

This personal and, at the time a secret, trauma helps us understand how much he wants the readers to identify with the Cratchits' poverty, and how this is not the fault of the family, but of the poor wages paid by Scrooge.

The next address he gives us is Scrooge's business in **"Cornhill"**. This is the financial centre of London. Miserly though Scrooge is with his own money, and misanthropic in his attitude to his fellow man, Scrooge still has to pay the going rate of **"fifteen"** shillings a week, and grant Bob a day's holiday at Christmas. Dickens' point is that Scrooge represents the financial city as a whole: London's wealth is based upon the exploitation of the poor, *who flood into the city from the surrounding countryside, so that applicants for any job are plentiful and business owners can keep wages very low.* This setting is essential to Dickens' message that Scrooge pays the same rate as any employer. This challenges his readers to ask if they too are unquestioningly paying the going rate and unintentionally keeping their employees in poverty.

The next city setting arrives when the Ghost of Christmas Yet to Come takes us to one of London's slums where the people are **"half naked, drunken, slipshod, ugly"** and they struggle to survive: **"the whole quarter reeked with crime, with filth, and misery"**. At first, the reader will assume the poor morals of the inhabitants has created the squalor they live in.

However, now Dickens presents **"the charwoman...laundress...and...undertaker's man"** who have stolen a pitiful hoard from Scrooge's corpse. The dealer in stolen goods, **"Old Joe"**, would dearly like to retire, but is forced to keep dealing in crime. He invites them into **"the parlour"**, which **"was the space behind the screen rags"**. Dickens portrays the slum as a setting which creates crime and criminals. Because he names the full-time occupations of the criminals, Dickens wants us to understand that they are actually driven to crime through poor wages, paid by Londoners who are exactly like Dickens' first readers.

He contrasts this with the upright Cratchit family trying desperately to make ends meet over a heartbreakingly small Christmas meal. This setting allows Scrooge to ask whether **"Tiny Tim will live"**, and the answer of course is no. Dickens' point is that morality is a luxury the poor cannot really afford. Tiny Tim dies because his family are honest, and because Scrooge pays the going rate. Dickens' deeper message is that moneyed society, and in particular London society, is to blame for the poverty and slums within it.

Just like Scrooge, Dickens' readers, have never visited these slums and seen the effects of the poor wages he pays to service people, so Dickens takes us "into an obscure part of the town, where Scrooge had never penetrated before". *Dickens visited many times in his nightly 15 to 20-mile walks, as he wrote the novel.* Dickens implies that his readers might have a different view of their moral responsibilities to their domestic staff and tradespeople if they saw the conditions in which they were forced to live.

However, because this novel is a comedy rather than a tragedy, Scrooge is redeemed, Tiny Tim does **"not die"**, And the cold bitterness of winter gives way: **"no fog, no mist; clear, bright, jovial, staring, cold… Golden sunlight."**

This particular adjective, **"Golden",** *is deliberately nostalgic. It is a deliberate reminder of the Ancient Greek myth of the Golden Age, a time of peace, harmony and prosperity. This is the world Dickens wants to recreate at Christmas, and the prosperity he wants to create all year.*

1160 words
963 words if you exclude the words in italic.

Your Turn: How is A Christmas Carol an Allegory or a Morality Play?

An allegory is a story in which the characters and events act as symbols. Jesus used these all the time to teach moral lessons: these allegories are called parables. The earliest English plays were allegories, in which all the characters represented different aspects of a person's character. These character traits battled between sinful desires and good Christian behaviour.

Most readers see **A Christmas Carol** as an allegorical morality tale.

1. **Deadly Sin of Greed:** Scrooge can be taken to represent the deadly sin of Greed (although I hope I have shown you that there is a much richer interpretation, and that he does not take pleasure from an excess of anything except control over his savings. He is essentially misanthropic).

2. **Christian Hope, the Christkindl:** The Ghost of Christmas Past, with its shape shifting from childhood form to that of an old man, represents the power of memory, and the effect of childhood on the man. It is also a symbol of Christian hope, in the way it mimics Christkindl. It's inextinguishable flame also represents the eternal life of the Christian soul in heaven.

3. **Pagan Traditions:** The Ghost of Christmas Present represents the true, pagan tradition of the Winter Solstice celebrations, fellowship, feasting, family and generosity toward the community and our fellow man.

4. **Memento Mori:** The Ghost of Christmas Yet to Come represents a Memento Mori, a fear not just of death, but of God's judgement. It symbolises moral judgement.

5. **The Working Poor:** The Cratchits symbolise the noble, struggling working classes, paid too little because there are so many poor people desperate for the same jobs. They symbolise the togetherness of families, love, and how to cope with everyday tragedy.

6. **Ignorance and Want:** symbolise the desperate need for education of the poor, and the dangers of society not looking after their needs. It is a warning of civil unrest and potential revolution. As children, they also symbolise Dickens hope that their future can be changed by a morally engaged reader.

7. **Belle:** can represent lost beauty and lost love, if we take the French meaning of her name. If we think of the symbolism of bells in the novel, we see that she also symbolises the tragic passing of time and how our relationships might be doomed from the start if we don't understand our patterns of attachment.

8. **Jacob Marley's Chain:** symbolises our past sins metaphorically encircling us. But they are specifically sins of misanthropy - seeing the poor as less worthy, perhaps even less human than yourself. This is what happens when we measure worth by monetary value.

434 Words for you to turn into a Grade 9 essay.

Top Quotations

Key

(These are the quotations taken from the essays you have just read, so you can see how useful they will be).

- **Bold** – the quotation is one I used in at least one of my seven essays
- **Bold and Yellow** – the quotation is relevant to many essays, so I've used it frequently

Preface

"I HAVE endeavoured in this Ghostly little book, to raise the **Ghost of an Idea**, which shall not put my readers out of humour with themselves, with each other, with the season, or with me. May it haunt their houses pleasantly"

Stave One

Scrooge

Scrooge never painted out **Old Marley's** name.

"workhouses … Are they still in operation?"

"Are there no prisons?"

"decrease the surplus population"

I don't make merry myself at Christmas and I can't afford to make **idle people** merry

"There's another fellow," muttered Scrooge; who overheard him: **"my clerk, with fifteen shillings a week**, and a wife and family, talking about a merry Christmas."

"Bah...Humbug!"

"carried his own low temperature always about with him"

"No warmth could warm"

"hard and sharp as flint"

Setting

"snow", "fog" and "cold"

"once upon a time"

"If we were not perfectly convinced that **Hamlet's Father** died before the play began…"

the clerk ... (for he boasted no great-coat), went down a slide on **Cornhill**, at the end of a lane of boys, twenty times, in honour of its being Christmas Eve, and then ran home to **Camden Town** as hard as he could pelt, to play at blindman's-buff.

Fred

"**why cannot we be friends?**"

Bob

"There's another fellow," muttered Scrooge; who overheard him: **"my clerk, with fifteen shillings a week**, and a wife and family, talking about a merry Christmas."

"If we were not perfectly convinced that **Hamlet's Father** died before the play began..."

"the clerk ... (for he boasted **no great-coat**), went **down a slide** on Cornhill, at the end of a lane of boys, **twenty times**, in honour of its being Christmas Eve, and then ran home to Camden Town as hard as he could pelt, **to play at blindman's-buff**."

Marley

"Scrooge never painted out **Old Marley's** name."

"That is no light part of my **penance**," pursued the Ghost. "I am here to-night to warn you, that you have yet a chance and hope of escaping **my fate. A chance and hope of my procuring, Ebenezer.**"

"Every one of them wore **chains like Marley's Ghost**; some few (they might be **guilty governments**) were linked together"

Stave Two

Scrooge

"**A solitary child, neglected by his friends**, is left there still."

"At one of these a lonely boy was reading near a feeble fire; and Scrooge sat down upon a form, and wept to see his **poor forgotten self** as he used to be."

"**Why, it's Ali Baba!**" Scrooge exclaimed in ecstasy. "It's dear old honest Ali Baba! Yes, yes, I know! One Christmas time, when **yonder solitary child** was left here all alone, **he did come**, for the first time, just like that. **Poor boy!**"

"Poor **Robin Crusoe**"

"when he thought that such another creature, quite as graceful and as full of promise, **might have called him father, and been a spring-time in the haggard winter of his life**" "**knew and named them** every one"

Setting

"snow"

Scrooge's Father

"Father is so much kinder than he used to be"

Fezziwig

He has the power to render us happy or unhappy; to make our service light or burdensome; a pleasure or a toil.

Stave Three

Ghost of Christmas Present

"It was clothed in one simple **green robe**, or mantle, bordered with white fur. This garment hung so loosely on the figure, that its capacious **breast was bare**"

"cramp these people's opportunities of innocent enjoyment...**deprive them of their means of dining every seventh day**".

"**sprinkled incense** on their dinners from his torch"

Scrooge

"if Tiny Tim will live"

The Cratchits

Martha: "We'd a deal of work to finish up last night," replied the girl, "and **had to clear away** this morning, mother!"

Mrs Cratchit: "dressed out but poorly in a twice-turned gown, **but brave in ribbons**"

Peter: "and getting the corners of his **monstrous shirt collar** (Bob's private property, conferred upon his son and heir in honour of the day) into his mouth, rejoiced to find himself so gallantly attired"

Bob: "his **threadbare clothes** darned up and brushed, to look seasonable"

Tiny Tim: that he hoped the people saw him **in the church**, because he was a **cripple**, and it might be pleasant to them to remember upon Christmas Day, **who made lame beggars walk**, and blind men see.

"there's **such** a goose,"

(surveying one **small atom of a bone** upon the dish)

"**if Tiny Tim will live**"

Fred

"I think I shook him yesterday"

"**to leave his poor clerk fifty pounds**"

"encouraged them in their merriment, and passed the **bottle joyously**."

"year after year"

"plump sister"

"they were so very confidential together, **behind the curtains**"

"**ring**" and "**chain**"

Ignorance and Want

"Yellow, meagre, **ragged**, scowling, **wolfish**"

"**Ignorance**" and "**Want**"

"but most of all **beware this boy**, for on his brow I see that written which is **Doom**, unless the writing be erased."

Ghost of Christmas Yet to Come

"beheld a solemn Phantom, **draped and hooded**..."

Stave Four

Ghost of Christmas Yet to Come

"The **Phantom** slowly, **gravely**, silently, approached."

Setting

"shrouded in a deep black garment"

"**the whole quarter reeked with crime, with filth, and misery**"

"They left the busy scene, and went into an **obscure part of the town**, where Scrooge had **never penetrated** before, although he recognised its situation, and its bad repute. The ways were foul and narrow; the shops and houses wretched; **the people half-naked, drunken, slipshod, ugly**."

Old Joe and the Working Criminals

"**nearly seventy years of age**"

"the parlour... the space behind the **screen of rags**."

"the **gallantry** of her friends"

"**laundress**" and "**charwoman**" and "**undertaker's man**"

"all three met here **without meaning it**!"

Tiny Tim and Bob

"**how patient and how mild**"

Stave Five

Setting

"**Golden sunlight**; Heavenly sky"

"**as Tiny Tim observed, God bless us every one**"

Fred

'"Is your **master** at home, my dear?" said Scrooge to the girl. Nice girl! Very.'

Scrooge

"and **to Tiny Tim, who did not die, he was a second father**."

"I am about to raise your salary!"

"their fill of laughter"

"He had no further intercourse with **Spirits**, but lived upon the **Total Abstinence Principle**, ever afterwards"

Other Quotations Teachers Like

Stave One Quotes

'Old Marley was as dead as a door-nail.'

'A merry Christmas, uncle! God save you!' cried a cheerful voice. It was the voice of Scrooge's nephew, who came upon him so quickly that this was the first intimation he had of his approach.

'Bah!' said Scrooge, 'Humbug!'

'Business!' cried the Ghost, wringing its hands again. 'Mankind was my business. The common welfare was my business; charity, mercy, forbearance, and benevolence, were, all, my business. The dealings of my trade were but a drop of water in the comprehensive ocean of my business!'

"Oh! but he was a tight-fisted hand at the grindstone, Scrooge! a squeezing, wrenching, grasping, scraping, clutching, covetous old sinner! Hard and sharp as flint, from which no steel had ever struck out generous fire; secret, and self-contained, and solitary as an oyster."

"'If they would rather die, . . . they had better do it, and decrease the surplus population.'"

Stave Two Quotes

It was a strange figure-like a child: yet not so like a child as like an old man, viewed through some supernatural medium, which gave him the appearance of having receded from the view, and being diminished to a child's proportions.

'The school is not quite deserted,' said the Ghost. **'A solitary child, neglected by his friends**, is left there still.'

'Our contract is an old one. It was made when we were both poor and content to be so, until, in good season, we could improve our worldly fortune by our patient industry. You are changed. When it was made, you were another man.'

Stave Three Quotes

In easy state upon this couch, there sat a jolly Giant, glorious to see, who bore a glowing torch, in shape not unlike Plenty's horn, and held it up, high up, to shed its light on Scrooge, as he came peeping round the door.

Oh, a wonderful pudding! Bob Cratchit said, and calmly too, that he regarded it as the greatest success achieved by Mrs Cratchit since their marriage: **"Everybody had something to say about it, but nobody said or thought it was at all a small pudding for a large family. It would have been flat heresy to do so.**

'God bless us every one!'"

Stave Four Quotes

The **Phantom** slowly, gravely, silently approached. When it came, Scrooge bent down upon his knee; for in the very air through which this Spirit moved it seemed to scatter gloom and mystery.

'Ghost of the Future!' he exclaimed, 'I fear you more than any spectre I have seen. But as I know your purpose is to do me good, and as I hope to live to be another man from what I was, I am prepared to bear you company, and do it with a thankful heart. Will you not speak to me?'

'If he wanted to keep them after he was dead, a wicked old screw,' pursued the woman, 'why wasn't he natural in his lifetime? If he had been, he'd have had somebody to look after him when he was struck with Death, instead of lying gasping out his last there, alone by himself.'

'He recoiled in terror, for the scene had changed, and now he almost touched a bed: a bare, uncurtained bed: on which, beneath a ragged sheet, there lay a something covered up, which, though it was dumb, announced itself in awful language.'

'Scrooge crept towards it, trembling as he went; and following the finger, read upon the stone of the neglected grave his own name, Ebenezer Scrooge.'

Stave Five Quotes

'I will live in the Past, the Present, and the Future!' Scrooge repeated, as he scrambled out of bed. 'The Spirits of all Three shall strive within me. Oh, Jacob Marley! Heaven, and the Christmas Time be praised for this! I say it on my knees, old Jacob, on my knees!'

'He went to church, and walked about the streets, and watched the people hurrying to and fro, and patted children on the head, and questioned beggars, and looked down into the kitchens of houses, and up to the windows, and found that everything could yield him pleasure. He had never dreamed that any walk – that anything – could give him so much happiness.'

Further Symbols

Light and Dark

Dickens presents light and dark in constant battle throughout the novel. He uses the word "light" 23 times, and it's opposite, "dark" 30 times. This is unexpected in what we imagine is an optimistic novel.

This contrast is particularly frequent in the portrayal of the ghosts. The Ghost of Christmas Past has "a bright clear jet of light". Remember that the imagery of its constantly changing body parts also feels macabre. Dickens adds to this by letting us know that this ghost is also associated with darkness, "at another time was dark, so the figure itself fluctuated in its distinctness", just as it fluctuates between youth and old age, "not so like a child as like an old man".

So, even the positive spiritual "light" of the ghost is threatened by its own darkness. This is a visual reminder of the Christian symbolism which sees mankind's battle between goodness and sin in each person's nature. This battle is typically described in terms of light and darkness.

You could argue that this ratio, where dark overpowers light, suggests that the optimistic ending of the novel is just for Christmas and that, once the festivities are over, life will return with a darker, more mean-spirited or tragic turn.

You could also argue that this also undermines our faith in Scrooge's conversion.

I prefer to argue the opposite. Scrooge represents how we can overcome what we feel is "dark" in our own lives - and those psychological causes of our own dark, negative habits. Dickens still paints a picture of a world where darkness is slightly stronger than light to illustrate how urgent it is that we redress the balance. The odds aren't overwhelming, and if his readers embrace the idea of paying higher wages, of thinking better of their fellow man, especially the poor, then that darkness can be overcome.

Dickens also uses The Ghost of Christmas Yet to Come to illustrate this. The first appearance of the ghost is as a Memento mori, emphasised through "shrouded", "black" and "darkness": "It was shrouded in a deep black garment, which concealed its head, its face, its form, and left nothing of it visible save one outstretched hand. But for this it would have been difficult to detach its figure from the night, and separate it from the darkness by which it was surrounded."

By the end of Stave Four, Scrooge's conversion has convinced the spirit to change into a "bedpost". Why? Perhaps this is because the darkness of sleep is restorative, a positive symbol. Similarly, Dickens stops referring to the ghost's "dark robe" at this point, and emphasises positive change in the phantom:

' "Good Spirit," he pursued, as down upon the ground he fell before it: "Your nature intercedes for me, and pities me. Assure me that I yet may change these shadows you have shown me, by an altered life!"

The kind hand trembled.'

Now the darkness has become only "shadows", and although shadows are made by light, we can symbolically "change" them by increasing light (at its brightest, when the sun is at midday, shadows are smallest).

Now, instead of being a reminder of death, the ghost is a reminder of hope, of "an altered life". Scrooge now sees the ghost as "Good Spirit" trying to help him by interceding with fate. Dickens suggests this transformation in Scrooge is real, that he has overcome the darkness of "these shadows", when the ghost is transformed to kindness: "The kind hand trembled".

Fog

Dickens uses the fog as pathetic fallacy. The fog's behaviour mirrors Scrooge's behaviour. So, at the beginning:

"The fog came pouring in at every chink and keyhole, and was so dense without, that although the court was of the narrowest, the houses opposite were mere phantoms. To see the dingy cloud come drooping down, obscuring everything, one might have thought that Nature lived hard by, and was brewing on a large scale."

Scrooge throws a similar blanket of negativity over Christmas. Interestingly, Dickens suggests that even the power of "Nature" is not strong enough to ruin the joy of Christmas. The houses may become "phantoms" in the "dense" fog, but Dickens uses the "phantoms" of Christmas to transform Scrooge.

By Stave Five, Scrooge has transformed and, in pathetic fallacy, the weather is also transformed. Symbolically, he removes the "fog": "No fog, no mist; clear, bright, jovial, stirring, cold; cold, piping for the blood to dance to; Golden sunlight; Heavenly sky; sweet fresh air; merry bells. Oh, glorious! Glorious!"

This symbolises how the power of Christmas transforms the oppressive power of "Nature" and winter, into the warm celebration of family and generosity.

Marley's Chain

The chain Marley wears symbolises his avarice (greed for money). This is clearly represented by the symbols of money and business attached to his chain: "cashboxes, keys, padlocks, ledgers, deeds, and heavy purses wrought in steel."

But Dickens also points out that all the other ghosts are wearing similar chains: "Every one of them wore chains like Marley's Ghost; some few (they might be guilty governments) were linked together; none were free."

This links all businessmen to avarice, so Dickens is suggesting that business, by its nature, makes life worse for their employees, keeping them poor. He also suggests that politicians are also to blame for poverty, by supposing that the ghosts who are linked by the same chain are "guilty governments".

Consequently, the chain isn't a simple Christian symbol, representing all the past sins of each ghost. For all of them, the sin is the same, creating poverty through low wages, and creating misery by not giving the poor the help they need instead of the "workhouse".

Interpretations

Patterns of Attachment Theory

R. Chris Fraley, Professor at the University of Illinois's Department of Psychology, summarises Attachment Theory:

> "individual differences in attachment representations are shaped by variation in experiences with caregivers in early childhood, and that, in turn, these early representations shape the quality of the individual's subsequent attachment experiences".

In other words, in our adult lives, we tend to reproduce the kinds of relationships we had with our parents.

This perfectly explains Scrooge's rejection of male friends, because he was so painfully rejected by his father. His one close male relationship is with another cold father figure, Jacob Marley. He too is older and will also abandon Scrooge through death.

This attachment also explains why Fezziwig, though a wonderful antidote and contrast to Scrooge's father, doesn't change Scrooge's behaviour (even though a nineteenth century apprenticeship lasted seven years).

The death of his mother, and then of Fan, are also kinds of abandonment, and also predict how he chooses Belle as a partner who is likely to abandon him, because of her age. It also predicts that his behaviour will unconsciously be calculated to alienate her and push her away, so that she will reproduce the pattern of abandonment.

The role of the Ghost of Christmas Past is to help Scrooge understand the effect of his past in creating the misanthropic miser he has become. Once Scrooge recognises that his adult relationships have reproduced the feelings and experience of being abandoned and rejected as a child, he can choose to break the pattern.

Capitalism

It is easy to see that the problems of poverty are created by capitalism. The Industrial Revolution has been a technological benefit of capitalism. But it has also led to jobs in cities and factories, which has in turn led to a huge increase in city populations. The number of houses in cities has not increased at the same rate, so more people are living in worse accommodation. Because there are many more opportunities in cities than the countryside, many more people flocked to the cities. This soon means there are many more people than jobs. This means that employers can pay very low wages, and still have lots of applicants for each job.

We have seen that Dickens constructs Bob Cratchit as a way to remind readers of their obligation to pay a living wage. He also reinforces that message through the charwoman, laundress and the undertaker's man.

However, the second problem with Scrooge's type of capitalism is his refusal to spend money within the economy. Thomas Malthus's gets a bad rap from English teachers. Far from wanting to kill off the poor, Malthus's main method of boosting the income of the poor was to encourage the well-off to spend. Spending money creates jobs, whereas simply paying higher wages might not lead to more job creation. Wages will increase the life expectancy and happiness of the working poor, not the unemployed poor. But spending, rather than holding on to money, will benefit the unemployed poor, because it will create more jobs. Dickens wants to tackle both inequalities.

This is why he makes Scrooge not just any kind of businessman, but a businessman who does not benefit the wider economy, because he has few employees and doesn't spend much at all in the economy.

Literary Context and Allusion

The Importance of Hamlet

Dickens begins the novel with a reference to Hamlet in the first few lines. This deliberately flatters a well-educated reader, who will be familiar with Shakespeare's play, but also helps us realise who the book is not aimed at: people without a very good education.

He also demand's some familiarity with the play's plot and jokes that Hamlet is a weak character with "a weak mind". This takes a play which was considered Shakespeare's greatest by Victorian audiences, and mocks the nature of its tragedy which revolves around a character, Hamlet, who simply can't make up his "weak mind". It lets us know that a main theme of this novel is going to be decisiveness, in thought and action.

Dickens also uses Hamlet's ghost to link the supernatural element of the ghost story to his major theme of fatherhood. This is why he calls the ghost "Hamlet's Father" and compares this to his "son". The beginning of the novel therefore announces that the father-son relationship is going to be crucial.

Hamlet's ghost is also in purgatory, seeking revenge for being murdered by his brother. He asks Hamlet to give him that revenge. Jacob has also been in a version of purgatory, but he blames himself for his ghostlike status. Instead of asking for revenge, he asks for redemption. Presumably, Dickens expects us to suppose that Marley will escape his purgatory if he is successful in helping Scrooge find his own redemption. Scrooge will escape his own purgatory in death if he redeems himself now in life, and becomes the new man of Stave Five.

A Time for Fun

Perhaps the greatest reason that this has been such a successful novel is Dickens' wonderful sense of fun. This is why he chooses a fun-loving narrator, who we laugh with and at in his descriptions. The narrator's outrageous appetite for food and for young women is supposed to amuse us and invite us to be a little critical of him, as we might good naturedly disapprove of a drunken relative at a Christmas gathering.

The ending shows Scrooge's playful delight. First, he sends a giant turkey anonymously, to astonish the Cratchits. Secondly, he pretends to be angry at Bob Cratchit for arriving late, having been slowed down by so much turkey the day before. Dickens himself revels in the comedy, describing how Bob Cratchit "a momentary idea of knocking Scrooge down with" a ruler, thinking he might have to defend himself physically from Scrooge's uncharacteristic generosity, believing that it is a sign of violent madness.

When Bob was released on Christmas Day, he ran back home with excitement. Dickens also reminds us that he might have been running because he had no coat to keep him warm. Yet he makes sure that Bob still stops to enjoy a slide with lots of other boys, and slides "twenty times".

As he gets home, he is excited about playing "blindman's buff".

Dickens also throws Scrooge, and us, into Fred's family fun, which is not just full of jokes about Scrooge as a "disagreeable animal", it also includes a game of blindman's buff which has been rigged in order to allow Fred's friend Topper to court one of Fred's sisters in law.

Christmas, therefore, becomes a celebration of fun as well as family. The narrator draws our attention to Fred's laughter, claiming there is no "man more blest in a laugh than Scrooge's nephew". He also points out Scrooge's new laugh at the end, where Scrooge laughs continuously, and "His own heart laughed" with joy. Laughter is at the heart of the novel, and also at the heart of the reader's experience.

Gothic Horror

This is not a gothic novel, because there is no supernatural mystery to be solved. Marley actually tells Scrooge he will be visited by three spirits, and exactly when they will arrive, at 1 am.

When Dickens creates the ghosts, he doesn't want to scare the reader. His preface makes clear that he wants to "haunt their houses pleasantly".

True, the Ghost of Christmas Yet to Come is a sinister figure, but as we'll see, he acts as a Memento mori. This symbolism is spiritual, a reminder to the need to live a Christian life. What terrifies Scrooge is not the "hooded" phantom, but the dead body which the reader has already worked out is Scrooge himself. He hears perhaps his own voice "Oh cold, cold, rigid, dreadful Death".

Even the first ghost, Marley, amuses as much as terrifies. Dickens introduces Marley's detachable jaw with a joke about the weather: "But how much greater was his horror, when the phantom taking off the bandage round its head, as if it were too warm to wear indoors, its lower jaw dropped down upon its breast!"

Key Vocabulary Explained

'Change - The Royal Exchange, the financial centre of London

"Nuts" to - If something is "Nuts" to someone, it pleases them. As in, 'she was nuts about fashion'. But it can also be a term of disdain and a refusal to do something. 'Homework? Nuts to that.'

counting-house – finance office

humbug - Nonsense

workhouses - Publicly institutions which took in those too poor to afford rent.

half a crown – 2.5 shillings, or 30 pence. One shilling was worth 12 pence.

great-coat – a large coat, made larger with a short cape on the shoulders

blindman's-buff – a popular parlour game. The player is blindfolded, then has to catch someone, anyone, and guess who it is by touch. You can imagine how important this game was as a way of flirting.

fancy - creative imagination

lumber-room – a room for storing wood and furniture

gruel - porridge

cravat - a fine scarf worn around the neck and tied in a bow

Marley's kerchief – wrapping which was tied around a corpse's head to keep the mouth closed.

apprenticed – a legal agreement where a boy worked for seven years for someone, in exchange for a salary and training in the trade or business.

Welsh wig – A woollen cap, originally made popular in Wales.

porter – a dark beer.

forfeits – popular parlour games in which play goes around the room. If a player makes a mistake or gives a wrong answer, they are penalised with a task as a punishment. Another great game for flirting.

Negus – alcohol wine, water, sugar, nutmeg, and, just to stop it being too sweet, lemon-juice.

Sir Roger de Coverley – a popular country dance, like our modern-day barn dances

cut – a jump in a dance, where feet land one in front of the other.

twelfth-cake - cakes celebrating Twelfth Night.

Bob - Slang for shilling, Cratchit earns 15 shillings a week, so 15 of his "Christian name".

twice-turned gown - mended

blood-horse - racehorse

copper - large tub normally used to boil laundry, used here to boil the pudding

twopence - two pennies, pronounced tuppence

five and sixpence - five shillings and six pennies, or five and a half shillings

milliner - maker of women's hats

menagerie - collection of wild animals

charwoman - a cleaning woman

poulterer - butcher who deals in fowl, mainly pheasants, geese, pigeon, chicken and turkey

Walk-ER - Cockney exclamation of disbelief, like chinny-right-on, you're having a giraffe; pull the other one, it's got bells on.

Joe Miller - Victorian comedian

smoking bishop – heated punch made from red wine, oranges, sugar, and spices. Bishops wore purple, hence the name

Printed in Great Britain
by Amazon